THE KINGFISHER

ATLAS OF THE MODERN WORLD

Simon Adams
Illustrated by Kevin Maddison

KINGFISHER
BOSTON

KINGFISHER

a Houghton Mifflin Company imprint
222 Berkeley Street
Boston, Massachusetts 02116
www.houghtonmifflinbooks.com

Senior editors: Simon Holland, Selina Wood
Coordinating editor: Caitlin Doyle
Designers: Rebecca Painter, Tony Cutting, Mike Davis
Cover designer: Neil Cobourne
Consultant: Professor Jeremy Black, University of Exeter, U.K.
Picture research manager: Cee Weston-Baker
Senior production controller: Jessamy Oldfield
DTP coordinator: Catherine Hibbert
DTP operator: Claire Cessford
Indexer: Clare Hibbert
Proofreader: Essie Cousins

Cartography by: Colin and Ian McCarthy
Maidenhead Cartographic Services Limited,
Maidenhead, Berkshire, U.K.

First published in 2007
2 4 6 8 10 9 7 5 3 1

1TR/0607/SHENS/SCHOY(SCHOY)/128MA/C

ISBN 978-0-7534-6034-4

LIBRARY OF CONGRESS CATALOGING-IN-PUBLICATION DATA
has been applied for.

Printed in Taiwan

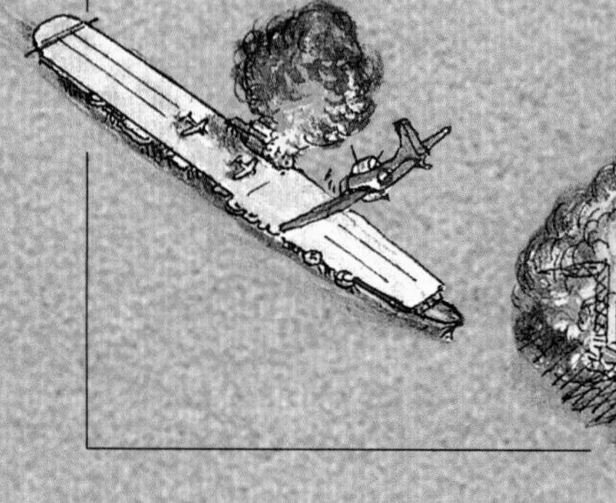

CONTENTS

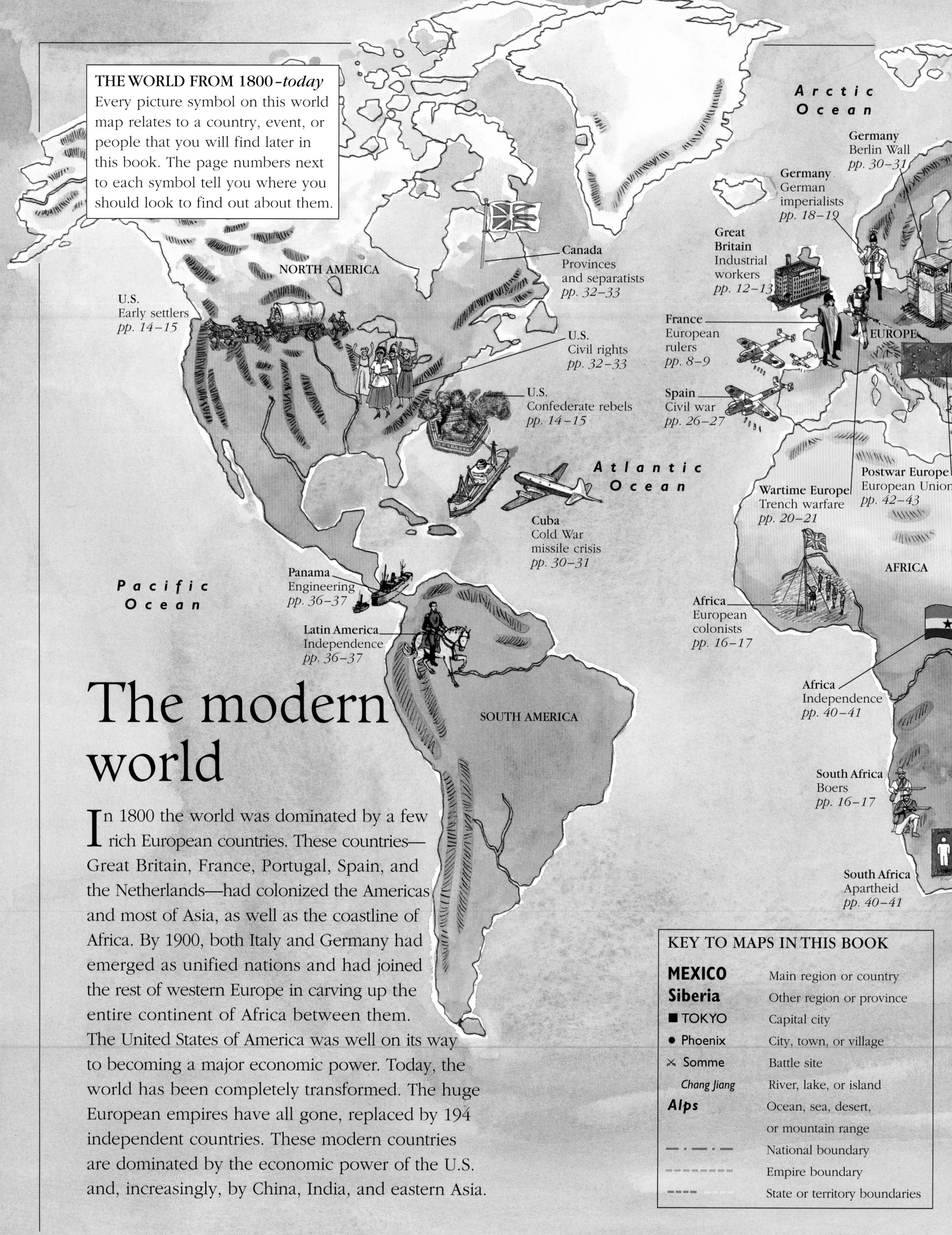
Arctic Ocean
Atlantic Ocean
Pacific Ocean
NORTH AMERICA
SOUTH AMERICA
EUROPE
AFRICA
Germany
Berlin Wall
pp. 30–31
Germany
German imperialists
pp. 18–19
Great Britain
Industrial workers
pp. 12–13
Canada
Provinces and separatists
pp. 32–33
U.S.
Early settlers
pp. 14–15
France
European rulers
pp. 8–9
U.S.
Civil rights
pp. 32–33
U.S.
Confederate rebels
pp. 14–15
Spain
Civil war
pp. 26–27
Postwar Europe
European Union
pp. 42–43
Wartime Europe
Trench warfare
pp. 20–21
Cuba
Cold War
missile crisis
pp. 30–31
Panama
Engineering
pp. 36–37
Latin America
Independence
pp. 36–37
Africa
European colonists
pp. 16–17
Africa
Independence
pp. 40–41
South Africa
Boers
pp. 16–17
South Africa
Apartheid
pp. 40–41

THE WORLD FROM 1800-*today*
Every picture symbol on this world map relates to a country, event, or people that you will find later in this book. The page numbers next to each symbol tell you where you should look to find out about them.

The modern world

In 1800 the world was dominated by a few rich European countries. These countries—Great Britain, France, Portugal, Spain, and the Netherlands—had colonized the Americas and most of Asia, as well as the coastline of Africa. By 1900, both Italy and Germany had emerged as unified nations and had joined the rest of western Europe in carving up the entire continent of Africa between them. The United States of America was well on its way to becoming a major economic power. Today, the world has been completely transformed. The huge European empires have all gone, replaced by 194 independent countries. These modern countries are dominated by the economic power of the U.S. and, increasingly, by China, India, and eastern Asia.

KEY TO MAPS IN THIS BOOK

MEXICO	Main region or country
Siberia	Other region or province
■ TOKYO	Capital city
• Phoenix	City, town, or village
⚔ Somme	Battle site
Chang Jiang	River, lake, or island
Alps	Ocean, sea, desert, or mountain range
— · — · —	National boundary
- - - - - -	Empire boundary
- - - -	State or territory boundaries

Russia
Revolutionaries
pp. 22–23
Russia
Freed serfs
pp. 18–19
Russia
Space travel
pp. 22–23
ASIA
Middle East
Oil wealth
pp. 38–39
China
Communists
pp. 34–35
Japan
Kamikaze pilots
pp. 28–29
Vietnam
Vietnam War
pp. 40–41
Pacific Ocean
India
Independence
pp. 40–41
Indian Ocean
AUSTRALIA
Australia
European settlers
pp. 12–13

LOCATOR MAP

You will find a world map like this with every map in the book. This allows you to see exactly which part of the world the main map is showing you.

POLITICAL MOVEMENTS

The following definitions may help you when reading this book:

CAPITALISM: An economic system based on private ownership, in which there is usually a free market to buy and sell goods.

COMMUNISM: A classless society in which private ownership is abolished. The means of production and subsistence belong to the community as a whole, although this system is often under the control of the state.

FASCISM: An extreme political movement based on nationalism (loyalty to one's country) and authority—often military—which aims to unite a country's people into a disciplined force under an all-powerful leader or dictator.

FUNDAMENTALISM: A movement that favors a very strict interpretation of any one religion and its scriptures or laws.

MARXISM: A movement based on the ideas of the philosopher Karl Marx (1818–1883), often known as the "father of communism."

NAZISM: A very extreme form of fascism, often involving highly racist policies.

1800–*today*

1800

1800 Act of Union unites Great Britain and Ireland
1804 Napoleon crowns himself the emperor of France
1807 Great Britain ends its involvement in the transatlantic slave trade
1815 Napoleon is defeated in Waterloo and sent into exile on Saint Helena
1821 Death of Napoleon

1825

1832 Greece gains independence from the Ottoman Empire
1834 Slaves freed throughout the British Empire
1839 Belgium gains independence from the Netherlands
1848–1849 Gold rush in California

1850

1859–1870 Italy is unified as one country
1861–1865 U.S. Civil War
1865 Slaves freed in the U.S.
1871 German Empire is created under Prussian leadership

1875

1877 Queen Victoria is proclaimed the empress of India
1884–1885 European countries agree to divide up Africa between them

1900

1905 Mass immigration to U.S. is at its peak
1911 Chinese republic is established
1914–1918 World War I
1917 Revolution in Russia creates world's first communist state, which later becomes the U.S.S.R.
1920 British Empire at its largest size
1921 Ireland becomes an independent state
1922 Mussolini takes power in Italy
1924 Stalin takes power in Russia

1925

1929 Collapse of the New York Stock Exchange leads to worldwide economic depression
1933 Hitler takes power in Germany
1936–1939 Spanish Civil War
1939–1945 World War II
1947 India and Pakistan become independent from British rule
1948 Creation of the state of Israel
1949 Communists take over China

1950

1953 Death of Stalin
1957 Treaty of Rome sets up the European Economic Community (EEC), later the EU
1957 First artificial satellite is sent into space
1957 Ghana becomes the first independent black African nation
1961–1963 John F. Kennedy is U.S. president
1962 Cuban missile crisis
1969 U.S. astronauts land on the Moon

1975

1979 Islamic revolution in Iran
1980 China begins massive economic expansion
1985 Gorbachev begins to reform the U.S.S.R.
1989–1990 Communism collapses across eastern Europe
1991 U.S.S.R. collapses and is replaced by 15 new countries; the Cold War ends
1994 Apartheid (enforced separation of blacks and whites) is abolished in South Africa

2000

2001 9/11 (September 11) terrorist attacks in the U.S.
2002 Single, unified currency introduced in 12 European nations within the European Union (EU)
2007 EU now has 27 member states

2025

The world since 1800:

An endlessly changing world

The pace of changes over the last 200 years has probably been greater than at any other time during human history. In 1800 the population of the world was around 930 million, and most of these people lived and worked on the land. Today, the world is home to around 6.4 billion people, the vast majority of whom live and work in increasingly overcrowded towns and cities. New industrial techniques, mass communication, and inventions such as the airplane and the computer have transformed the lives of almost everyone today, while few people have been able to escape the effects of the wars and conflicts that have raged around the globe during the last century.

Industrial change
The Industrial Revolution began in Great Britain in the late 1700s and spread throughout Europe and across to the United States during the 1800s. Millions of people who had previously worked on the land or in small workshops now lived and worked in large industrial towns. They worked long hours in factories, iron and steel works, and shipyards—as in New York City (above)—where the working conditions were often difficult and dangerous.

The impact of war
The 1900s was one of the most brutal periods in all of human history. Two major world wars and several other conflicts killed millions of people and transformed the lives of millions more. For example, women worked in jobs that had been previously undertaken only by men such as in heavy industrial plants (left). In many countries women also gained the right to vote and to be treated as equals to men for the first time.

Into space
The first human-made satellite to orbit Earth, *Sputnik 1*, was launched in 1957. Twelve years later astronauts landed on the Moon, and by the end of the century, they lived and worked in space for months at a time in space stations that orbited far above Earth's surface (below). Unmanned spacecraft have now explored the farthest planets, sending back remarkable photographs of our solar system and beyond.

The International Space Station (ISS) is made up of separate modules, which have been launched into space individually since 1998.

Space shuttle astronauts perform spacewalks to connect together the different modules.

Communication

The development of the telegraph, postal services, mass printing techniques, the telephone, radio, television, and the Internet have transformed communication over the last 200 years. This also means that we have a huge volume of historical evidence to tell us about this period—photographs, printed material such as newspapers, and film and sound recordings. Today, information can be spread around the world in seconds via satellite technology, while computers are rapidly transforming the way that we work, study, and entertain ourselves.

abcNEWS
EXTENDED INTERVIEW

Television set from the 1960s

Early 20th-century telephone

Modern laptop computer

Cellular telephone with a digital camera

Newspapers are still an important source of up-to-date information. They are now printed and distributed at great speed, and in huge quantities, thanks to automated printing presses such as this one (above).

Napoleonic Europe

In 1804 Napoleon Bonaparte, the ruler of France since 1799 and the most successful military leader of his time, crowned himself Emperor Napoleon I. A series of incredible victories gained him control of most of Europe, with only Great Britain able to resist him. In 1812 he invaded Russia in a final attempt to end Russian opposition to his rule. Although he seized the capital, Moscow, he was forced to retreat because of the fierce Russian winter. Victories turned to defeats, and in 1815 a joint British and Prussian force finally overcame Napoleon in Waterloo.

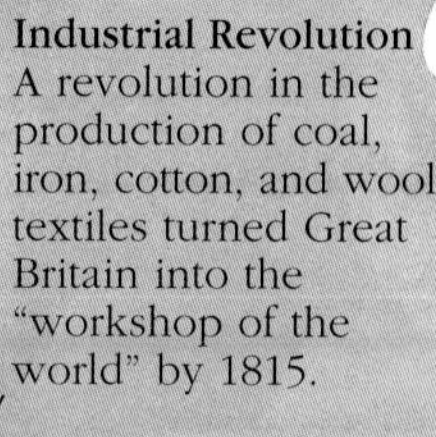
Scotland
Ireland
Dublin
GREAT BRITAIN
LONDON
North Sea
DENMARK
NETHERLANDS
GERMAN STATES
Boulogne
Waterloo
Rhine
Amiens
PARIS
FRANCE
Ulm
SWITZERLAND
ALPS
Atlantic Ocean
PORTUGAL
SPAIN
MADRID
LISBON
Vitoria
Trafalgar
Balearic Islands
Corsica
Sardinia
ALGIERS

Industrial Revolution
A revolution in the production of coal, iron, cotton, and wool textiles turned Great Britain into the "workshop of the world" by 1815.

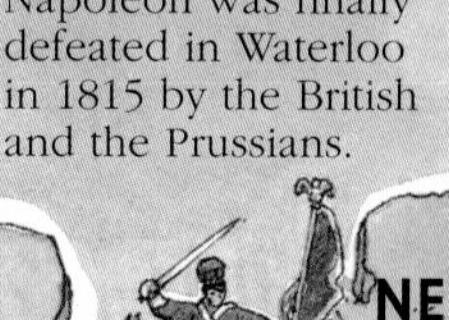

Battle of Waterloo
Napoleon was finally defeated in Waterloo in 1815 by the British and the Prussians.

The Great Reform Act
The British parliament was reformed in 1832 to make it more fair and less corrupt.

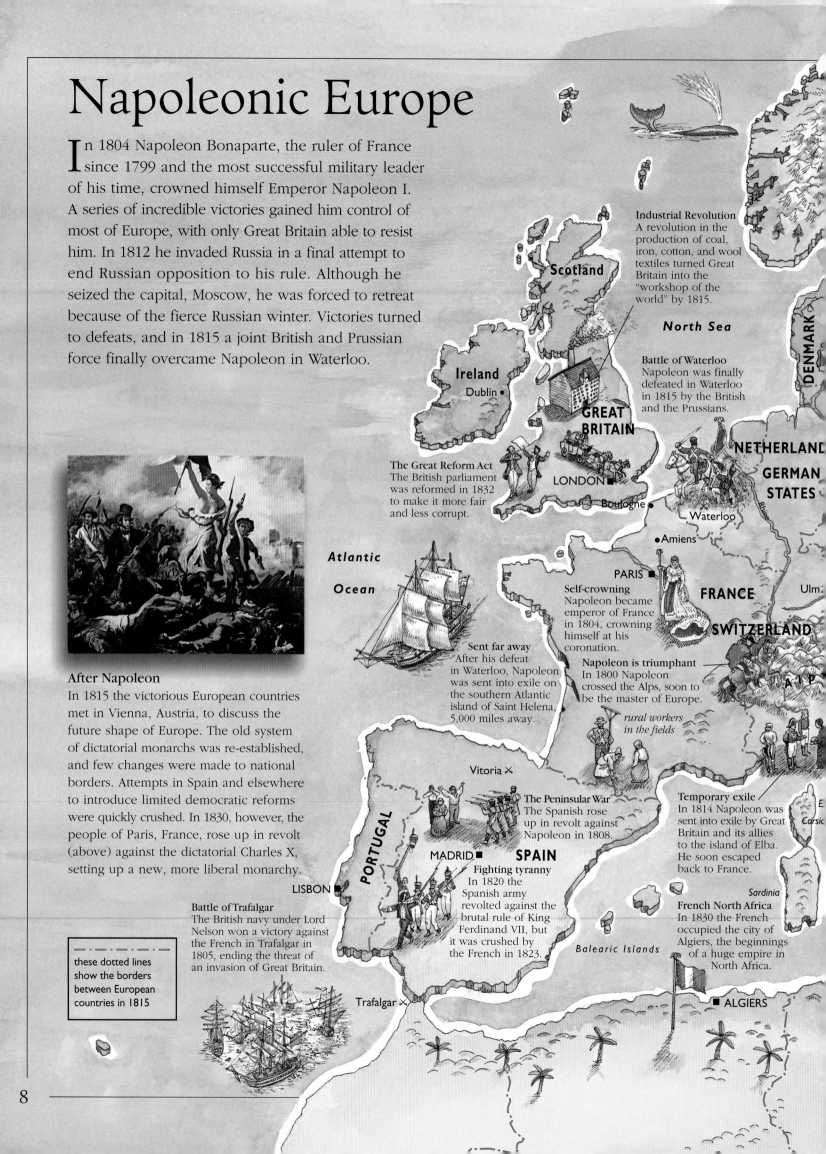

After Napoleon
In 1815 the victorious European countries met in Vienna, Austria, to discuss the future shape of Europe. The old system of dictatorial monarchs was re-established, and few changes were made to national borders. Attempts in Spain and elsewhere to introduce limited democratic reforms were quickly crushed. In 1830, however, the people of Paris, France, rose up in revolt (above) against the dictatorial Charles X, setting up a new, more liberal monarchy.

Self-crowning
Napoleon became emperor of France in 1804, crowning himself at his coronation.

Sent far away
After his defeat in Waterloo, Napoleon was sent into exile on the southern Atlantic island of Saint Helena, 5,000 miles away.

Napoleon is triumphant
In 1800 Napoleon crossed the Alps, soon to be the master of Europe.

rural workers in the fields

The Peninsular War
The Spanish rose up in revolt against Napoleon in 1808.

Temporary exile
In 1814 Napoleon was sent into exile by Great Britain and its allies to the island of Elba. He soon escaped back to France.

Fighting tyranny
In 1820 the Spanish army revolted against the brutal rule of King Ferdinand VII, but it was crushed by the French in 1823.

French North Africa
In 1830 the French occupied the city of Algiers, the beginnings of a huge empire in North Africa.

Battle of Trafalgar
The British navy under Lord Nelson won a victory against the French in Trafalgar in 1805, ending the threat of an invasion of Great Britain.

– · – · – · –
these dotted lines show the borders between European countries in 1815

Moscow burning
After their victory in Borodino in 1812, the French occupied Moscow and burned most of it to the ground.
MOSCOW
Borodino
WEDEN
openhagen
Tilsit
Friedland
Retreat from Moscow
The severe Russian winter forced Napoleon's army to retreat from Russia in 1812, suffering massive losses as the troops headed home.
0
500km
0
250 miles
RUSSIAN EMPIRE
Berlin
PRUSSIA
Leipzig
Battle of Austerlitz
Napoleon defeated the Russians and the Austrians in Austerlitz on December 2, 1805.
Austerlitz
ARIA
Wagram
VIENNA
Serbs revolt
The Serbs revolted against their Ottoman rulers, winning home rule in 1817.
Moldavia
AUSTRIAN EMPIRE
Black Sea
Ottoman Empire
Although this empire was in decline, the sultan still ruled most of southeast Europe, North Africa, and the Middle East.
Wallachia
Danube
Serbia
OTTOMAN EMPIRE
PAPAL STATES
CONSTANTINOPLE
Greeks rebel
The Greeks rose up in revolt against their Ottoman rulers in 1821. They gained independence in 1832.
Naples
INGDOM OF THE 'O SICILIES
Young Italy
The Young Italy movement, founded in 1831, fought for a united republic of Italy.
ATHENS
GREECE
Navarino
Battle of Navarino
A combined British, French, and Russian fleet destroyed an Ottoman fleet in Navarino in 1827, helping the Greeks win their independence.
Mediterranean Sea

1800–1840

1800

1802 Great Britain and France sign the peace treaty of Amiens

1803 Great Britain and France go to war again; Napoleon prepares to invade Great Britain

1804 Napoleon becomes the emperor of Europe; he applies the "Code Napoléon" (French civil law) across Europe

1805 The Austrians and Russians are beaten in Austerlitz; the British navy defeats the French in Trafalgar, ending the threat of invasion

1807 The Russians and Prussians are defeated in Friedland

1808 Peninsular War begins in Spain—a lengthy conflict is fought by the Spanish and British against French occupation

1810

1812 Napoleon invades Russia, but the harsh winter forces troops to retreat

1813 The British under Wellington defeat the French in Vitoria, Spain, ending the Peninsular War; Napoleon is defeated by Russians, Austrians, and Prussians at the "Battle of the Nations" in Leipzig

1814 As enemies threaten Paris, France, Napoleon is forced to abdicate and is exiled to Elba

1815 Napoleon escapes from Elba but is finally defeated in Waterloo and is sent into exile again

1815 Congress of Vienna redraws the maps of Europe and restores previous kingdoms: Norway is united with Sweden and Belgium with the Netherlands

1817 Serbia wins home rule from Ottoman Empire

1820

1820 Revolutions are crushed in Portugal and Naples

1820–1823 Spanish revolt against Ferdinand VII is ended by the French

1821 Napoleon dies on Saint Helena in the southern Atlantic Ocean

1821 The Greeks begin war of independence against Ottoman rule

1827 Anglo-French-Russian fleet defeats Ottoman-Egyptian fleet in Navarino

1829 Moldavia and Wallachia win home rule from the Ottoman Empire

1830

1830 Revolution in France: King Charles X is overthrown and replaced by Louis-Philippe

1830 French occupy Algiers

1830–1831 Revolutions are crushed in Italy and Poland

1830–1839 Belgian revolt against Dutch rule leads to Belgian independence

1831 Young Italy movement is founded

1832 Great Reform Act is passed in Great Britain

1832 Greece becomes an independent monarchy

1840

Industrial Revolution:

Steam, iron, and steel

The railroads

The need to move raw materials to factories and take away their finished products led to a revolution in transportation. A network of canals was built in Great Britain after the 1760s, but it was the invention of the railroads in the early 1800s that led to the biggest changes. The first American steam railroad opened in 1830. Fifty years later there were more railroads in the U.S. (above) than in all of Europe.

An industrial revolution began in Great Britain during the 1760s. New machines, driven by steam and water, were used to manufacture textiles and other products in factories that were manned by hundreds of workers. Steam engines hauled coal and iron out of mines and powered railroad engines to transport raw materials and finished goods. New technologies transformed the production of iron, steel, and chemicals. The revolution transformed Great Britain—and later the rest of Europe and the U.S.—from a mostly rural society into an urban one. New industrial towns, where the workers lived, were often squalid. Before long, people began to campaign for social and political reforms to improve these living conditions.

Industrial towns

The development of factories led to the rapid growth of many towns such as Leeds in northern England (shown below). Living conditions in these towns were often terrible, as new houses for the workers were built back-to-back and close to the factories, mills, and mines where they worked.

Smoke from factories' chimneys darkened the sky and polluted the water supply

Nearby farms were quickly swamped by the expanding towns

Workers lived in cramped housing with few amenities

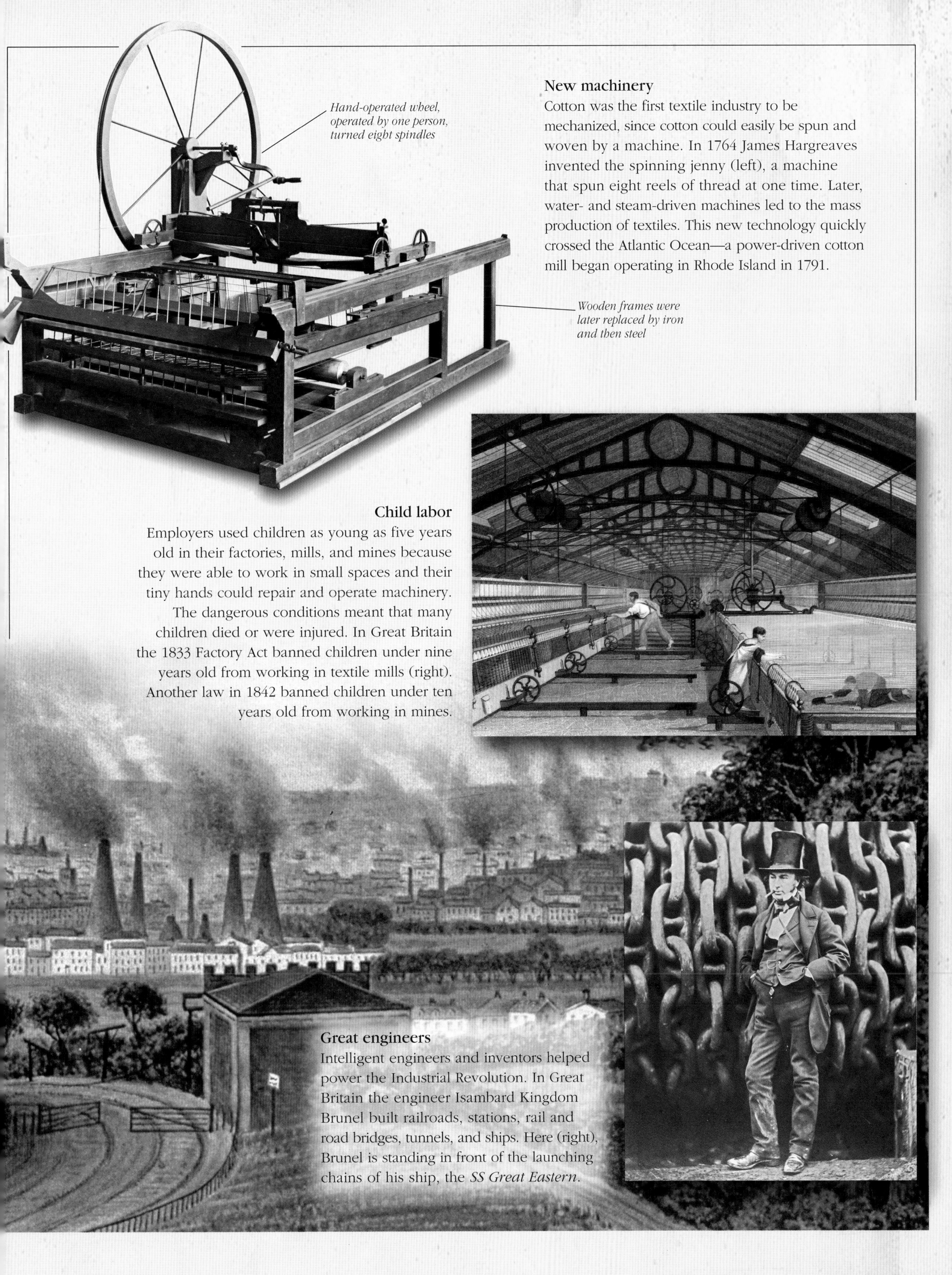
Hand-operated wheel, operated by one person, turned eight spindles
Wooden frames were later replaced by iron and then steel

New machinery

Cotton was the first textile industry to be mechanized, since cotton could easily be spun and woven by a machine. In 1764 James Hargreaves invented the spinning jenny (left), a machine that spun eight reels of thread at one time. Later, water- and steam-driven machines led to the mass production of textiles. This new technology quickly crossed the Atlantic Ocean—a power-driven cotton mill began operating in Rhode Island in 1791.

Child labor

Employers used children as young as five years old in their factories, mills, and mines because they were able to work in small spaces and their tiny hands could repair and operate machinery. The dangerous conditions meant that many children died or were injured. In Great Britain the 1833 Factory Act banned children under nine years old from working in textile mills (right). Another law in 1842 banned children under ten years old from working in mines.

Great engineers

Intelligent engineers and inventors helped power the Industrial Revolution. In Great Britain the engineer Isambard Kingdom Brunel built railroads, stations, rail and road bridges, tunnels, and ships. Here (right), Brunel is standing in front of the launching chains of his ship, the *SS Great Eastern*.

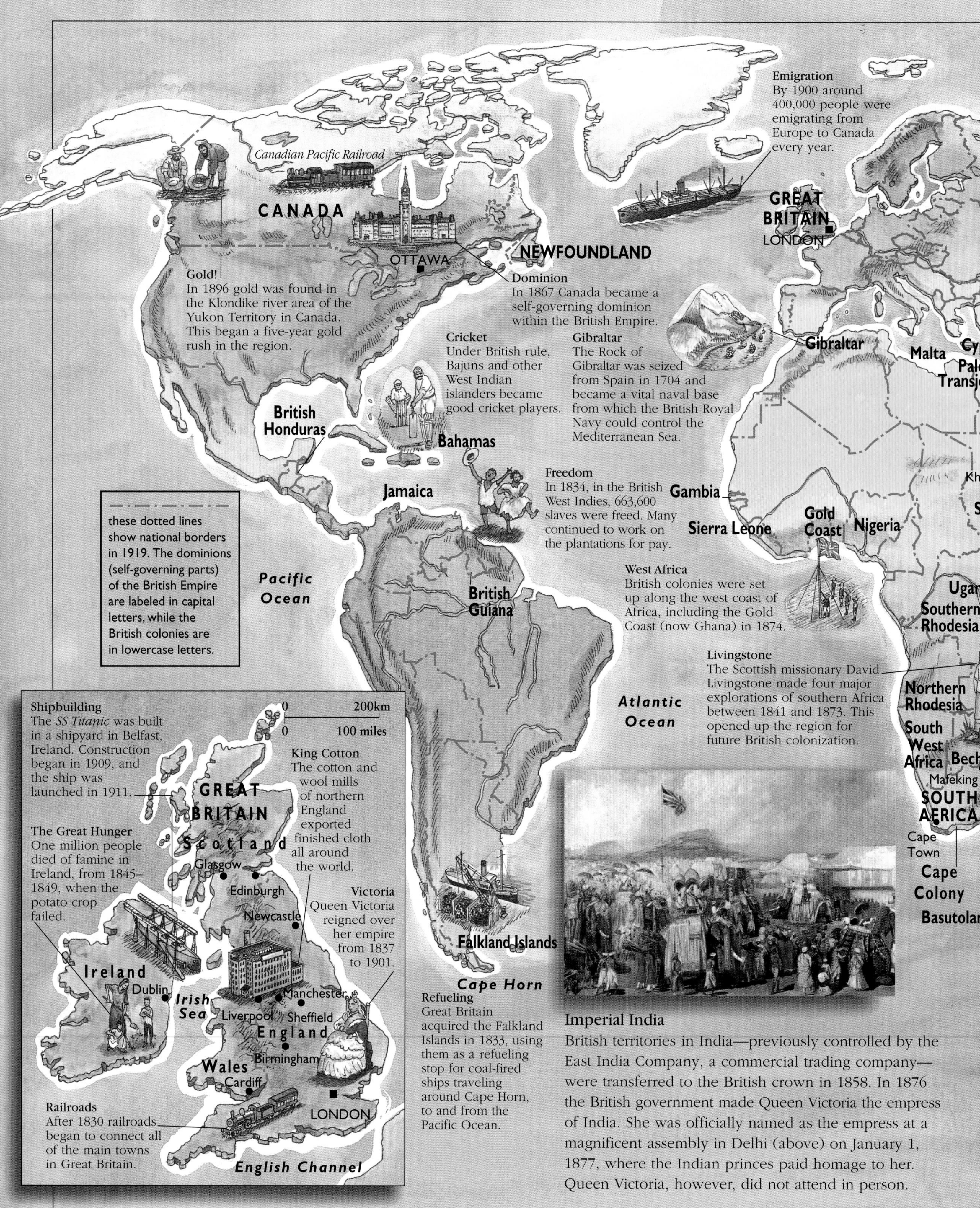
Emigration
By 1900 around 400,000 people were emigrating from Europe to Canada every year.
Canadian Pacific Railroad
CANADA
GREAT BRITAIN
LONDON
OTTAWA
NEWFOUNDLAND
Gold!
In 1896 gold was found in the Klondike river area of the Yukon Territory in Canada. This began a five-year gold rush in the region.
Dominion
In 1867 Canada became a self-governing dominion within the British Empire.
Cricket
Under British rule, Bajuns and other West Indian islanders became good cricket players.
Gibraltar
The Rock of Gibraltar was seized from Spain in 1704 and became a vital naval base from which the British Royal Navy could control the Mediterranean Sea.
Gibraltar
Malta
British Honduras
Bahamas
Freedom
In 1834, in the British West Indies, 663,600 slaves were freed. Many continued to work on the plantations for pay.
Jamaica
Gambia
Sierra Leone
Gold Coast
Nigeria
these dotted lines show national borders in 1919. The dominions (self-governing parts) of the British Empire are labeled in capital letters, while the British colonies are in lowercase letters.
Pacific Ocean
British Guiana
West Africa
British colonies were set up along the west coast of Africa, including the Gold Coast (now Ghana) in 1874.
Uganda
Southern Rhodesia
Livingstone
The Scottish missionary David Livingstone made four major explorations of southern Africa between 1841 and 1873. This opened up the region for future British colonization.
Atlantic Ocean
Northern Rhodesia
South West Africa
Mafeking
SOUTH AFRICA
Cape Town
Cape Colony
Basutoland
Shipbuilding
The SS Titanic was built in a shipyard in Belfast, Ireland. Construction began in 1909, and the ship was launched in 1911.
0 200km
0 100 miles
King Cotton
The cotton and wool mills of northern England exported finished cloth all around the world.
GREAT BRITAIN
Scotland
The Great Hunger
One million people died of famine in Ireland, from 1845–1849, when the potato crop failed.
Glasgow
Edinburgh
Newcastle
Victoria
Queen Victoria reigned over her empire from 1837 to 1901.
Ireland
Dublin
Irish Sea
Manchester
Liverpool
Sheffield
England
Wales
Birmingham
Cardiff
LONDON
Railroads
After 1830 railroads began to connect all of the main towns in Great Britain.
English Channel
Falkland Islands
Cape Horn
Refueling
Great Britain acquired the Falkland Islands in 1833, using them as a refueling stop for coal-fired ships traveling around Cape Horn, to and from the Pacific Ocean.

Imperial India

British territories in India—previously controlled by the East India Company, a commercial trading company—were transferred to the British crown in 1858. In 1876 the British government made Queen Victoria the empress of India. She was officially named as the empress at a magnificent assembly in Delhi (above) on January 1, 1877, where the Indian princes paid homage to her. Queen Victoria, however, did not attend in person.

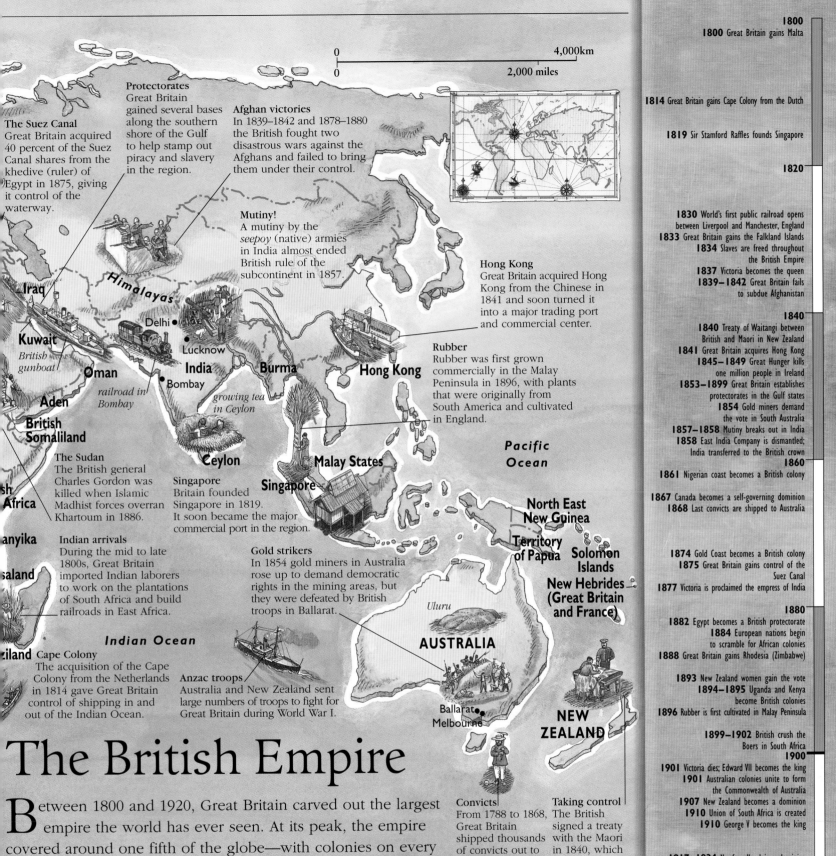

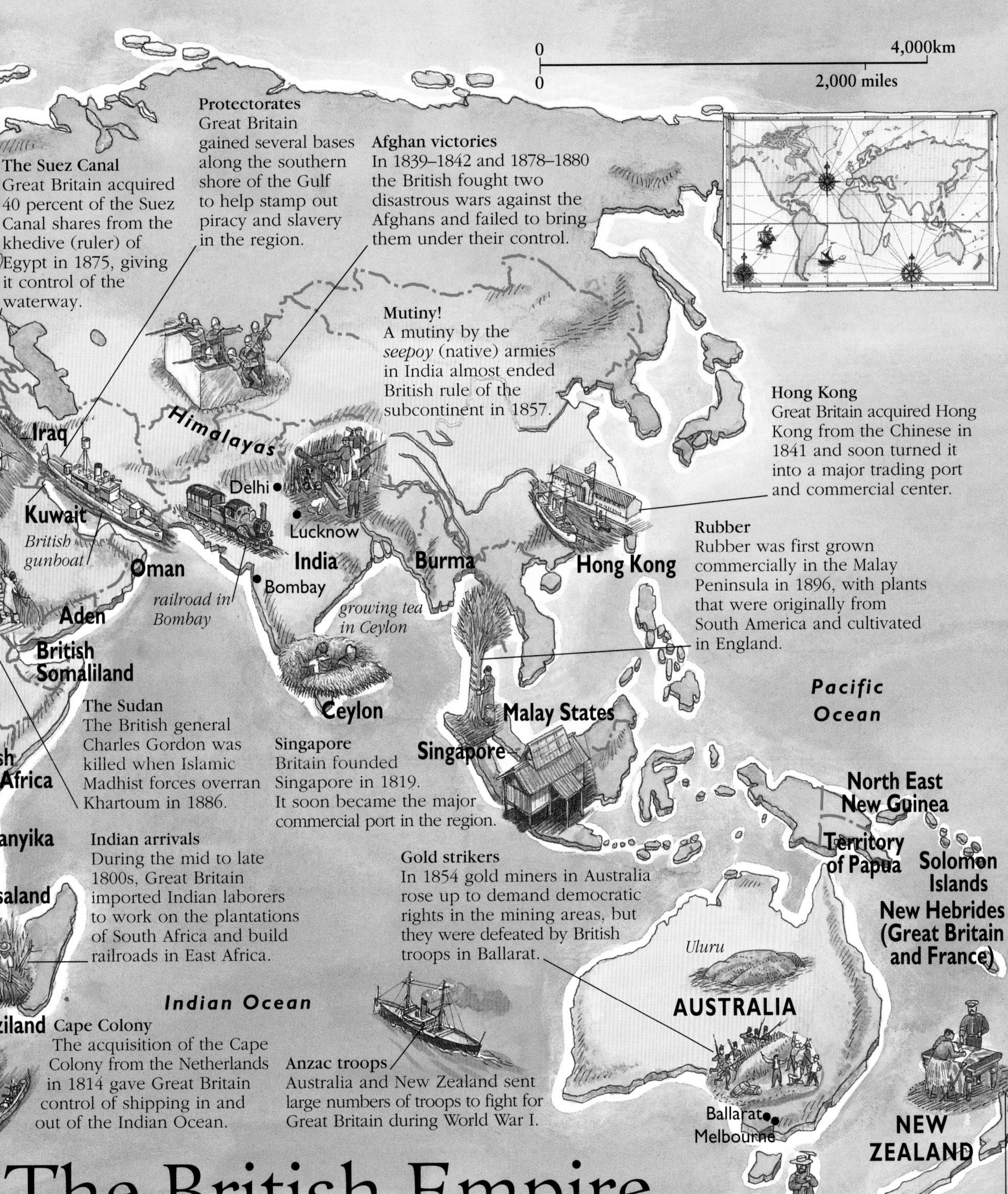

0
4,000km
0
2,000 miles
The Suez Canal
Great Britain acquired 40 percent of the Suez Canal shares from the khedive (ruler) of Egypt in 1875, giving it control of the waterway.
Protectorates
Great Britain gained several bases along the southern shore of the Gulf to help stamp out piracy and slavery in the region.
Afghan victories
In 1839–1842 and 1878–1880 the British fought two disastrous wars against the Afghans and failed to bring them under their control.
Mutiny!
A mutiny by the *seepoy* (native) armies in India almost ended British rule of the subcontinent in 1857.
Hong Kong
Great Britain acquired Hong Kong from the Chinese in 1841 and soon turned it into a major trading port and commercial center.
Himalayas
Iraq
Delhi
Lucknow
Kuwait
British gunboat
Oman
India
Burma
Hong Kong
Bombay
railroad in Bombay
Aden
growing tea in Ceylon
British Somaliland
Rubber
Rubber was first grown commercially in the Malay Peninsula in 1896, with plants that were originally from South America and cultivated in England.
Pacific Ocean
The Sudan
The British general Charles Gordon was killed when Islamic Madhist forces overran Khartoum in 1886.
Ceylon
Malay States
Singapore
Singapore
Britain founded Singapore in 1819. It soon became the major commercial port in the region.
North East New Guinea
Territory of Papua
Solomon Islands
New Hebrides (Great Britain and France)
Indian arrivals
During the mid to late 1800s, Great Britain imported Indian laborers to work on the plantations of South Africa and build railroads in East Africa.
Gold strikers
In 1854 gold miners in Australia rose up to demand democratic rights in the mining areas, but they were defeated by British troops in Ballarat.
Uluru
AUSTRALIA
Indian Ocean
Cape Colony
The acquisition of the Cape Colony from the Netherlands in 1814 gave Great Britain control of shipping in and out of the Indian Ocean.
Anzac troops
Australia and New Zealand sent large numbers of troops to fight for Great Britain during World War I.
Ballarat
Melbourne
NEW ZEALAND

The British Empire

Between 1800 and 1920, Great Britain carved out the largest empire the world has ever seen. At its peak, the empire covered around one fifth of the globe—with colonies on every continent—and contained 410 million people, one fifth of the world's population. The British built the empire in order to provide raw materials for their industries—such as cotton, silk, sugar, gold, and diamonds—and a ready market for finished goods. It also defended vital British shipping and commercial interests around the world. Pride in British values, as well as a desire to convert local people to Christianity, were also the reasons for the creation of the empire.

Convicts
From 1788 to 1868, Great Britain shipped thousands of convicts out to Australia to serve their sentences in penal colonies.

Taking control
The British signed a treaty with the Maori in 1840, which gave Great Britain control of New Zealand.

1800–1940

1800
1800 Great Britain gains Malta
1814 Great Britain gains Cape Colony from the Dutch
1819 Sir Stamford Raffles founds Singapore
1820
1830 World's first public railroad opens between Liverpool and Manchester, England
1833 Great Britain gains the Falkland Islands
1834 Slaves are freed throughout the British Empire
1837 Victoria becomes the queen
1839–1842 Great Britain fails to subdue Afghanistan
1840
1840 Treaty of Waitangi between British and Maori in New Zealand
1841 Great Britain acquires Hong Kong
1845–1849 Great Hunger kills one million people in Ireland
1853–1899 Great Britain establishes protectorates in the Gulf states
1854 Gold miners demand the vote in South Australia
1857–1858 Mutiny breaks out in India
1858 East India Company is dismantled; India transferred to the British crown
1860
1861 Nigerian coast becomes a British colony
1867 Canada becomes a self-governing dominion
1868 Last convicts are shipped to Australia
1874 Gold Coast becomes a British colony
1875 Great Britain gains control of the Suez Canal
1877 Victoria is proclaimed the empress of India
1880
1882 Egypt becomes a British protectorate
1884 European nations begin to scramble for African colonies
1888 Great Britain gains Rhodesia (Zimbabwe)
1893 New Zealand women gain the vote
1894–1895 Uganda and Kenya become British colonies
1896 Rubber is first cultivated in Malay Peninsula
1899–1902 British crush the Boers in South Africa
1900
1901 Victoria dies; Edward VII becomes the king
1901 Australian colonies unite to form the Commonwealth of Australia
1907 New Zealand becomes a dominion
1910 Union of South Africa is created
1910 George V becomes the king
1917–1934 Newfoundland is a dominion
1919 Great Britain, Australia and New Zealand gain German colonies in Africa and Oceania
1920
1920 Great Britain gains Iraq, Jordan, and Palestine—the empire is at its largest size
1922 Ireland becomes a Free State within the British Empire
1922 Egypt becomes independent
1931 Statute of Westminster makes dominions independent and equal to Great Britain and creates the British Commonwealth of Nations
1936 George VI becomes the king after his brother, Edward VIII, abdicates
1939 The empire joins Great Britain in World War II against Germany, Italy, and, in 1941, Japan
1940

The U.S. in the 1800s

In just over 100 years, the United States of America transformed itself. It grew from a narrow strip of newly independent colonies along the coast of the Atlantic Ocean to a continental power that stretched out across the Pacific Ocean and up toward the Arctic. However, most of this new land was already occupied by Native Americans, who fought fiercely to survive and keep their ancient heritage alive. By the end of the 1800s, the Native Americans were confined to special reservations, and the U.S. was on its way to becoming the richest and most powerful country in the world.

The U.S. Civil War
The southern states of the U.S. allowed white citizens to keep black slaves to work on their cotton plantations and in their homes. However, other states were against slavery. The argument between the two sides erupted in 1861, when 11 southern states left the Union and set up the independent Confederacy. A vicious civil war broke out that lasted for four years and killed at least 600,000 people. This picture shows Confederate fortifications close to Petersburg, Virginia, in 1865. The Union, led by President Abraham Lincoln, eventually won the war and abolished slavery.

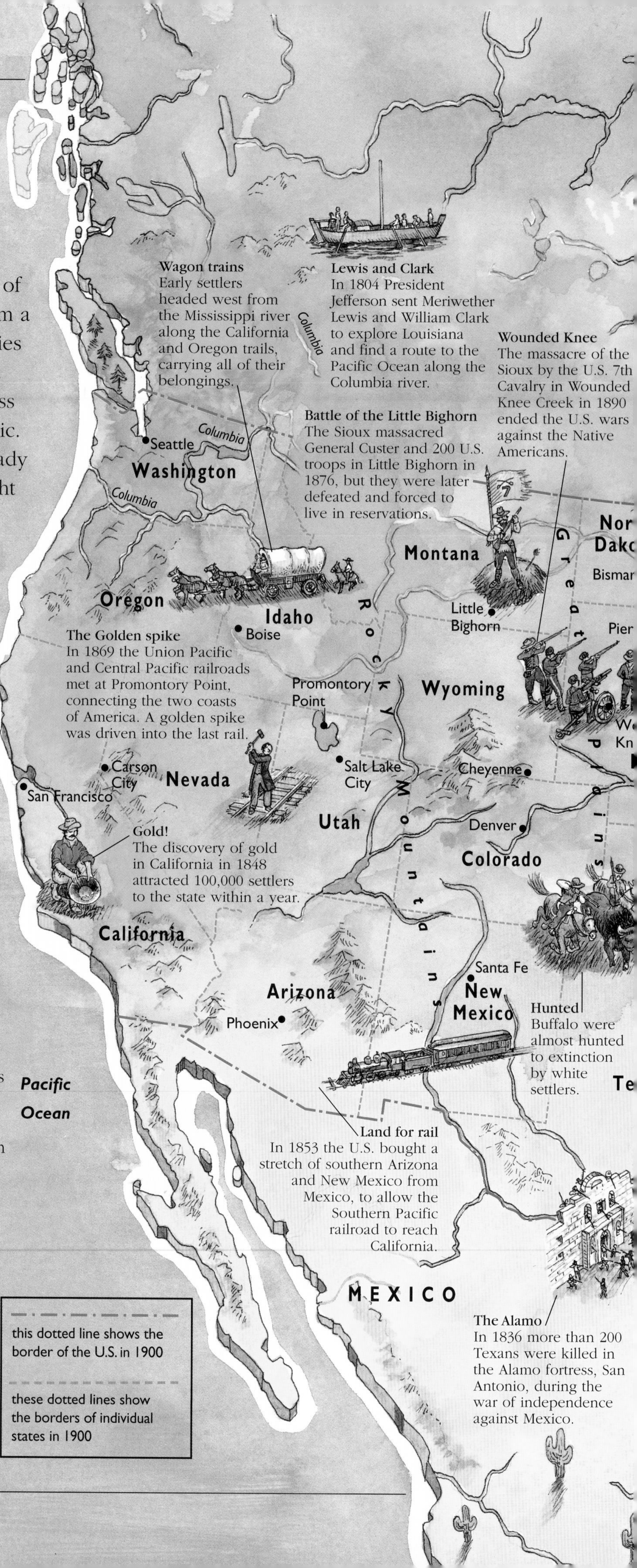

Wagon trains
Early settlers headed west from the Mississippi river along the California and Oregon trails, carrying all of their belongings.

Lewis and Clark
In 1804 President Jefferson sent Meriwether Lewis and William Clark to explore Louisiana and find a route to the Pacific Ocean along the Columbia river.

Wounded Knee
The massacre of the Sioux by the U.S. 7th Cavalry in Wounded Knee Creek in 1890 ended the U.S. wars against the Native Americans.

Battle of the Little Bighorn
The Sioux massacred General Custer and 200 U.S. troops in Little Bighorn in 1876, but they were later defeated and forced to live in reservations.

The Golden spike
In 1869 the Union Pacific and Central Pacific railroads met at Promontory Point, connecting the two coasts of America. A golden spike was driven into the last rail.

Gold!
The discovery of gold in California in 1848 attracted 100,000 settlers to the state within a year.

Hunted
Buffalo were almost hunted to extinction by white settlers.

Land for rail
In 1853 the U.S. bought a stretch of southern Arizona and New Mexico from Mexico, to allow the Southern Pacific railroad to reach California.

The Alamo
In 1836 more than 200 Texans were killed in the Alamo fortress, San Antonio, during the war of independence against Mexico.

Washington
Seattle
Columbia
Oregon
Idaho
Boise
Montana
Little Bighorn
Wyoming
Promontory Point
Salt Lake City
Cheyenne
Nevada
Carson City
San Francisco
Utah
Denver
Colorado
California
Arizona
Phoenix
Santa Fe
New Mexico
Rocky Mountains
Great Plains
Pacific Ocean
MEXICO

this dotted line shows the border of the U.S. in 1900

these dotted lines show the borders of individual states in 1900

0 — 1,000km
0 — 500 miles

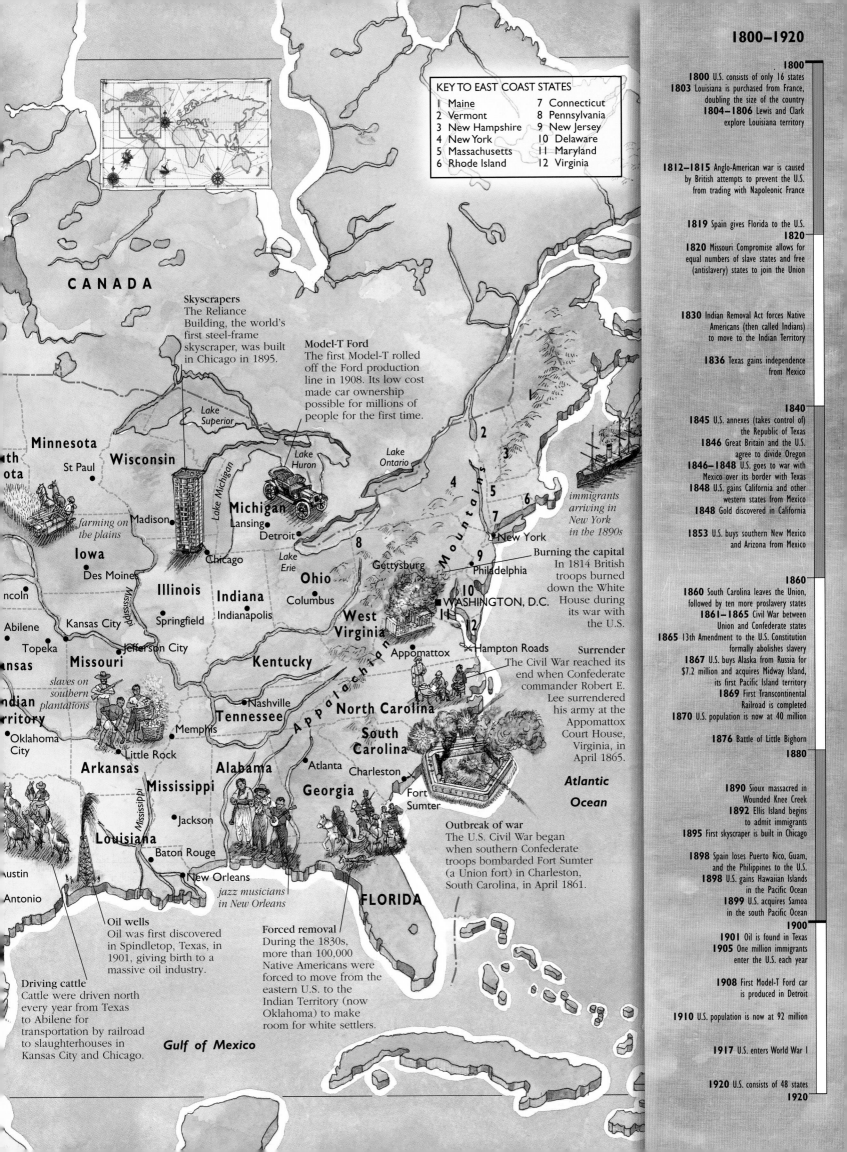

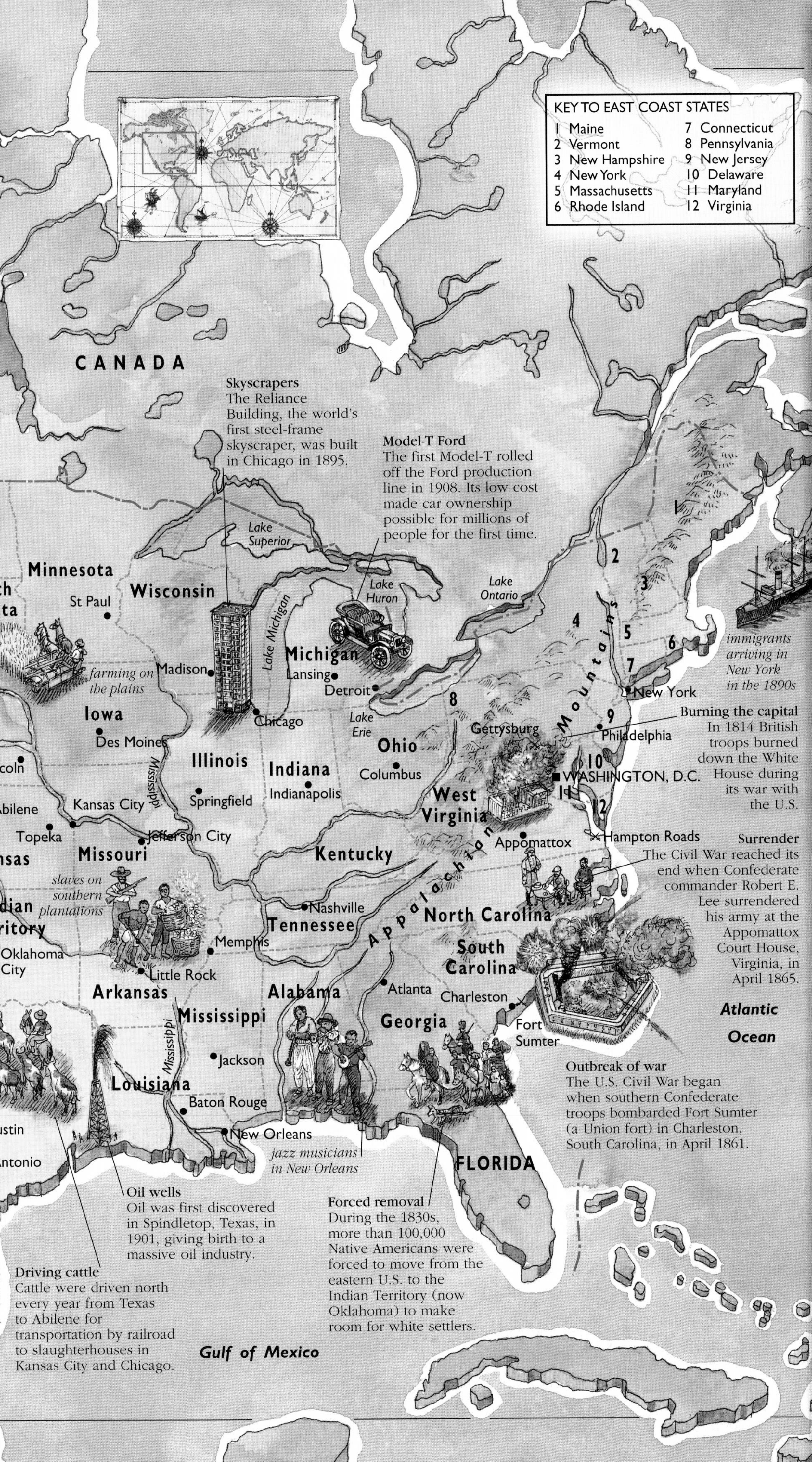
KEY TO EAST COAST STATES
1 Maine
2 Vermont
3 New Hampshire
4 New York
5 Massachusetts
6 Rhode Island
7 Connecticut
8 Pennsylvania
9 New Jersey
10 Delaware
11 Maryland
12 Virginia
CANADA
Skyscrapers
The Reliance Building, the world's first steel-frame skyscraper, was built in Chicago in 1895.
Model-T Ford
The first Model-T rolled off the Ford production line in 1908. Its low cost made car ownership possible for millions of people for the first time.
Lake Superior
Lake Huron
Lake Ontario
Lake Michigan
Lake Erie
Minnesota
St Paul
Wisconsin
farming on the plains
Madison
Michigan
Lansing
Detroit
Iowa
Des Moines
Chicago
Illinois
Indiana
Ohio
Columbus
Springfield
Indianapolis
Kansas City
Abilene
Topeka
Jefferson City
Missouri
Mississippi
Kentucky
West Virginia
Appalachian Mountains
Gettysburg
Philadelphia
New York
immigrants arriving in New York in the 1890s
Burning the capital
In 1814 British troops burned down the White House during its war with the U.S.
WASHINGTON, D.C.
Appomattox
Hampton Roads
Surrender
The Civil War reached its end when Confederate commander Robert E. Lee surrendered his army at the Appomattox Court House, Virginia, in April 1865.
slaves on southern plantations
Nashville
Tennessee
North Carolina
South Carolina
Memphis
Oklahoma City
Little Rock
Arkansas
Alabama
Atlanta
Charleston
Georgia
Fort Sumter
Mississippi
Jackson
Louisiana
Baton Rouge
New Orleans
jazz musicians in New Orleans
Atlantic Ocean
Outbreak of war
The U.S. Civil War began when southern Confederate troops bombarded Fort Sumter (a Union fort) in Charleston, South Carolina, in April 1861.
FLORIDA
Oil wells
Oil was first discovered in Spindletop, Texas, in 1901, giving birth to a massive oil industry.
Forced removal
During the 1830s, more than 100,000 Native Americans were forced to move from the eastern U.S. to the Indian Territory (now Oklahoma) to make room for white settlers.
Driving cattle
Cattle were driven north every year from Texas to Abilene for transportation by railroad to slaughterhouses in Kansas City and Chicago.
Gulf of Mexico

1800–1920

1800

1800 U.S. consists of only 16 states
1803 Louisiana is purchased from France, doubling the size of the country
1804–1806 Lewis and Clark explore Louisiana territory

1812–1815 Anglo-American war is caused by British attempts to prevent the U.S. from trading with Napoleonic France

1819 Spain gives Florida to the U.S.

1820

1820 Missouri Compromise allows for equal numbers of slave states and free (antislavery) states to join the Union

1830 Indian Removal Act forces Native Americans (then called Indians) to move to the Indian Territory

1836 Texas gains independence from Mexico

1840

1845 U.S. annexes (takes control of) the Republic of Texas
1846 Great Britain and the U.S. agree to divide Oregon
1846–1848 U.S. goes to war with Mexico over its border with Texas
1848 U.S. gains California and other western states from Mexico
1848 Gold discovered in California

1853 U.S. buys southern New Mexico and Arizona from Mexico

1860

1860 South Carolina leaves the Union, followed by ten more proslavery states
1861–1865 Civil War between Union and Confederate states
1865 13th Amendment to the U.S. Constitution formally abolishes slavery
1867 U.S. buys Alaska from Russia for $7.2 million and acquires Midway Island, its first Pacific Island territory
1869 First Transcontinental Railroad is completed
1870 U.S. population is now at 40 million

1876 Battle of Little Bighorn

1880

1890 Sioux massacred in Wounded Knee Creek
1892 Ellis Island begins to admit immigrants
1895 First skyscraper is built in Chicago

1898 Spain loses Puerto Rico, Guam, and the Philippines to the U.S.
1898 U.S. gains Hawaiian Islands in the Pacific Ocean
1899 U.S. acquires Samoa in the south Pacific Ocean

1900

1901 Oil is found in Texas
1905 One million immigrants enter the U.S. each year

1908 First Model-T Ford car is produced in Detroit

1910 U.S. population is now at 92 million

1917 U.S. enters World War I

1920 U.S. consists of 48 states

1920

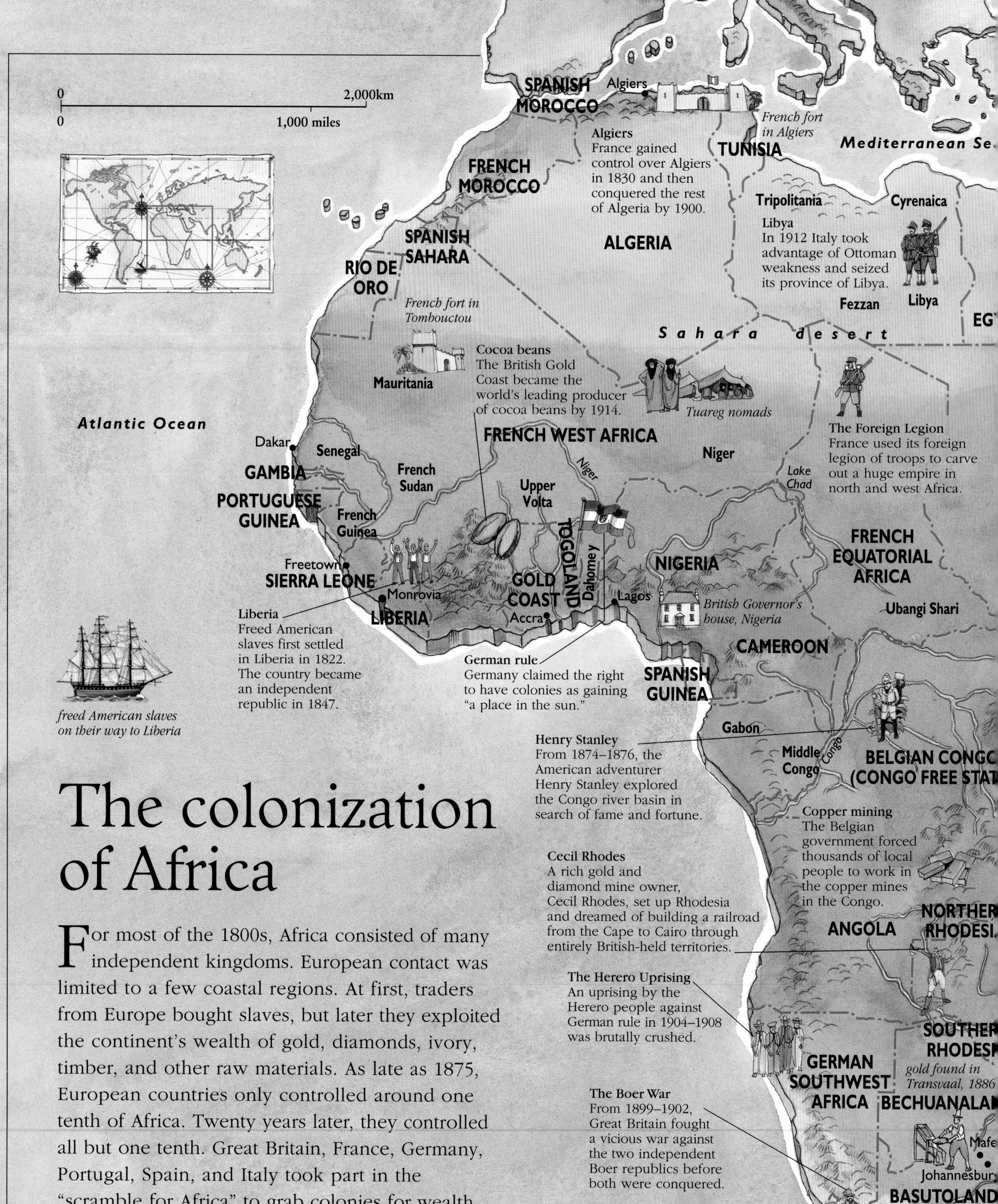

0
2,000km
0
1,000 miles
SPANISH MOROCCO
Algiers
French fort in Algiers
Algiers
France gained control over Algiers in 1830 and then conquered the rest of Algeria by 1900.
TUNISIA
Mediterranean Se
FRENCH MOROCCO
Tripolitania
Cyrenaica
Libya
In 1912 Italy took advantage of Ottoman weakness and seized its province of Libya.
SPANISH SAHARA
RIO DE ORO
ALGERIA
Fezzan
Libya
EG
French fort in Tombouctou
Sahara desert
Cocoa beans
The British Gold Coast became the world's leading producer of cocoa beans by 1914.
Mauritania
Tuareg nomads
Atlantic Ocean
FRENCH WEST AFRICA
The Foreign Legion
France used its foreign legion of troops to carve out a huge empire in north and west Africa.
Dakar
Senegal
GAMBIA
French Sudan
Niger
Niger
Lake Chad
Upper Volta
PORTUGUESE GUINEA
French Guinea
TOGOLAND
Dahomey
FRENCH EQUATORIAL AFRICA
Freetown
SIERRA LEONE
NIGERIA
GOLD COAST
Monrovia
Lagos
British Governor's house, Nigeria
Ubangi Shari
LIBERIA
Accra
Liberia
Freed American slaves first settled in Liberia in 1822. The country became an independent republic in 1847.
CAMEROON
German rule
Germany claimed the right to have colonies as gaining "a place in the sun."
SPANISH GUINEA
freed American slaves on their way to Liberia
Gabon
Henry Stanley
From 1874–1876, the American adventurer Henry Stanley explored the Congo river basin in search of fame and fortune.
Middle Congo
Congo
BELGIAN CONGO (CONGO FREE STAT
Copper mining
The Belgian government forced thousands of local people to work in the copper mines in the Congo.
Cecil Rhodes
A rich gold and diamond mine owner, Cecil Rhodes, set up Rhodesia and dreamed of building a railroad from the Cape to Cairo through entirely British-held territories.
ANGOLA
NORTHER RHODESI
The Herero Uprising
An uprising by the Herero people against German rule in 1904–1908 was brutally crushed.
SOUTHER RHODES
GERMAN SOUTHWEST AFRICA
gold found in Transvaal, 1886
BECHUANALA
The Boer War
From 1899–1902, Great Britain fought a vicious war against the two independent Boer republics before both were conquered.
Mafe
Johannesbur
BASUTOLAND
UNION OF SOUTH AFRICA
The Great Trek
Boer farmers escaped from British rule in the Cape Colony by moving north in the Great Trek of 1834–1848. They settled in what became the Orange Free State and Transvaal.
Cape Town
Cape Colony

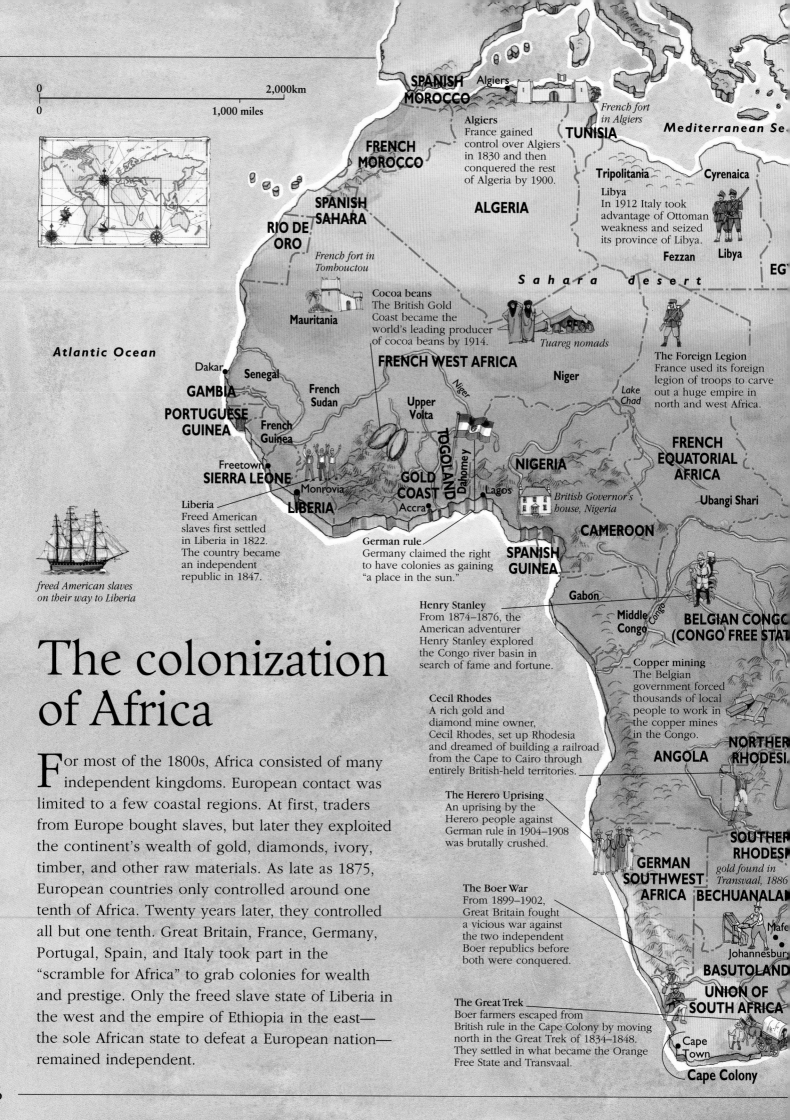

The colonization of Africa

For most of the 1800s, Africa consisted of many independent kingdoms. European contact was limited to a few coastal regions. At first, traders from Europe bought slaves, but later they exploited the continent's wealth of gold, diamonds, ivory, timber, and other raw materials. As late as 1875, European countries only controlled around one tenth of Africa. Twenty years later, they controlled all but one tenth. Great Britain, France, Germany, Portugal, Spain, and Italy took part in the "scramble for Africa" to grab colonies for wealth and prestige. Only the freed slave state of Liberia in the west and the empire of Ethiopia in the east—the sole African state to defeat a European nation—remained independent.

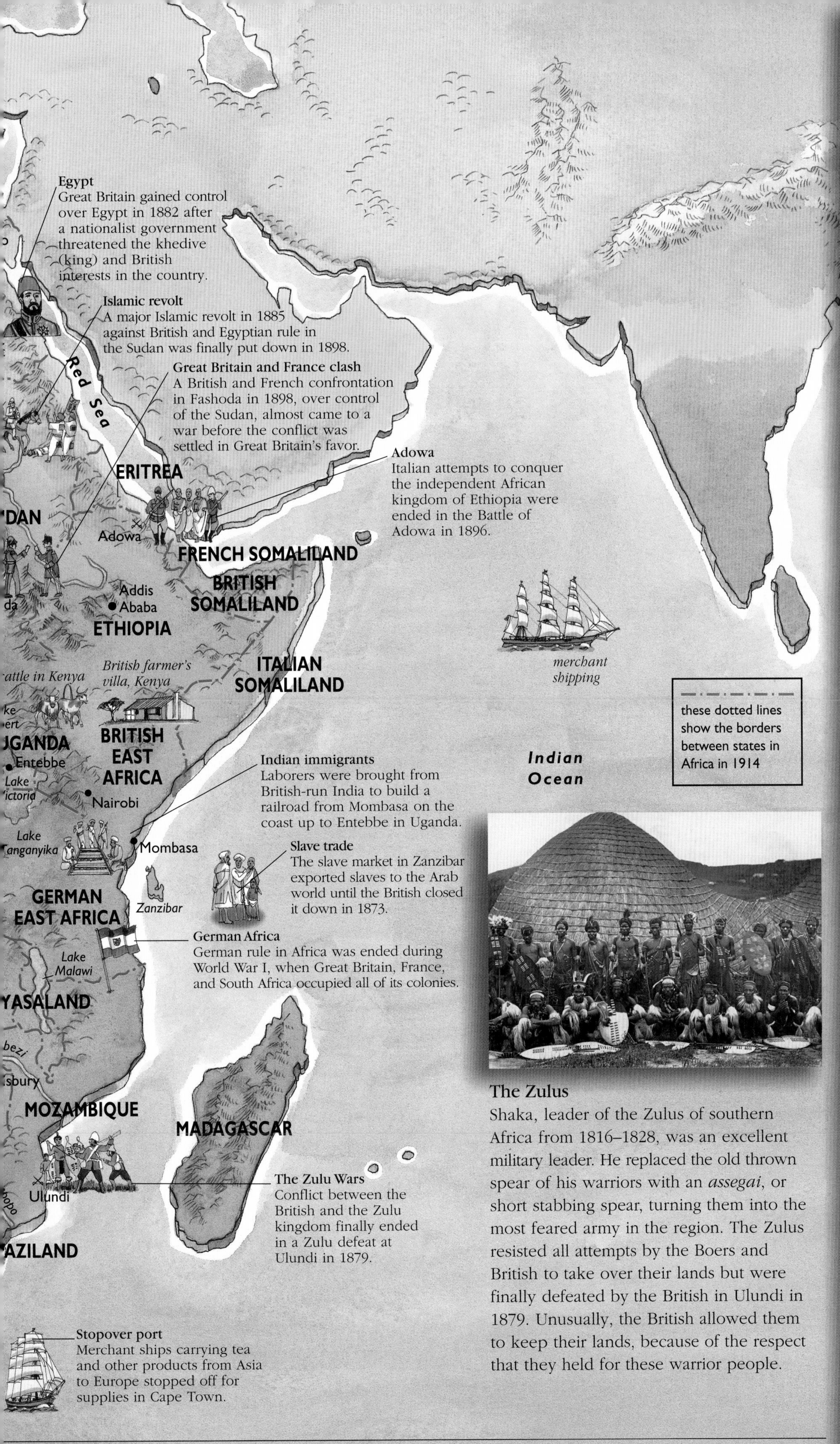

Egypt
Great Britain gained control over Egypt in 1882 after a nationalist government threatened the khedive (king) and British interests in the country.

Islamic revolt
A major Islamic revolt in 1885 against British and Egyptian rule in the Sudan was finally put down in 1898.

Great Britain and France clash
A British and French confrontation in Fashoda in 1898, over control of the Sudan, almost came to a war before the conflict was settled in Great Britain's favor.

Adowa
Italian attempts to conquer the independent African kingdom of Ethiopia were ended in the Battle of Adowa in 1896.

Indian immigrants
Laborers were brought from British-run India to build a railroad from Mombasa on the coast up to Entebbe in Uganda.

Slave trade
The slave market in Zanzibar exported slaves to the Arab world until the British closed it down in 1873.

German Africa
German rule in Africa was ended during World War I, when Great Britain, France, and South Africa occupied all of its colonies.

The Zulu Wars
Conflict between the British and the Zulu kingdom finally ended in a Zulu defeat at Ulundi in 1879.

Stopover port
Merchant ships carrying tea and other products from Asia to Europe stopped off for supplies in Cape Town.

Red Sea
ERITREA
DAN
Adowa
FRENCH SOMALILAND
BRITISH SOMALILAND
Addis Ababa
ETHIOPIA
ITALIAN SOMALILAND
British farmer's villa, Kenya
attle in Kenya
GANDA
BRITISH EAST AFRICA
Entebbe
Lake Victoria
Nairobi
Lake Tanganyika
Mombasa
GERMAN EAST AFRICA
Zanzibar
Lake Malawi
YASALAND
MOZAMBIQUE
MADAGASCAR
Ulundi
AZILAND
merchant shipping
Indian Ocean
these dotted lines show the borders between states in Africa in 1914

The Zulus

Shaka, leader of the Zulus of southern Africa from 1816–1828, was an excellent military leader. He replaced the old thrown spear of his warriors with an *assegai*, or short stabbing spear, turning them into the most feared army in the region. The Zulus resisted all attempts by the Boers and British to take over their lands but were finally defeated by the British in Ulundi in 1879. Unusually, the British allowed them to keep their lands, because of the respect that they held for these warrior people.

1800–1925

1800

1807 British end their involvement in the transatlantic slave trade

1814 Great Britain gains Cape Colony from the Dutch

1822 First freed slaves settle in Liberia

1825

1826 Great Britain begins to take over the Gold Coast

1830 France invades Algiers

1830–1900 France conquers Algeria

1834–1848 Boers move north in the Great Trek

1840–1873 David Livingstone explores central Africa

1847 Liberia becomes an independent republic

1850

1852–1854 Boers establish the republics of Orange Free State and Transvaal

1854 France takes over Senegal

1855 Emperor Tewedros begins to modernize Ethiopia

1861 Great Britain begins to colonize Nigeria

1873 British end the slave market in Zanzibar

1874–1876 Henry Stanley explores the Congo river region

1875

1879 British finally conquer the Zulu kingdom

1882 British take control of Egypt

1884–1885 European powers divide up Africa at the Berlin Conference

1885 Leopold II of Belgium makes the Congo his personal possession

1885–1898 Islamic revolt by the Mahdi against British rule in Sudan

1886 Gold discovered in the Transvaal

1888 British establish Rhodesia

1889 Italy gains Eritrea and Somaliland

1894 Great Britain occupies Uganda

1895 Great Britain occupies Kenya

1896 Italians fail to conquer Ethiopia

1898 Great Britain retakes Sudan

1899–1902 British defeat the Boers in South Africa

1900

1904 Great Britain and France settle their colonial disputes in Africa

1904–1908 Herero Uprising against German rule in southwest Africa

1906 Morocco is split between France and Spain

1908 Belgium takes control of the Congo

1910 Union of South Africa gains independence from Great Britain

1914–1918 Germany loses its African colonies during World War I

1925

Imperial Europe

In the years after 1848 the map of Europe changed significantly. Germany and Italy emerged as unified countries, and Austro-Hungary became a dual monarchy. France became an empire again and then, after 1871, a republic, while Russia slowly began to reform itself. Great Britain, the most powerful and richest country in the world, avoided European entanglements and developed a huge overseas empire. In the Balkans the Ottoman (Turkish) Empire continued to fall apart, losing almost all of its European land by 1913. The Industrial Revolution that had begun in Great Britain led to new industries and railroads in most countries, creating new industrial towns and a large working class population.

HMS Dreadnought
The battleship *Dreadnought* outclassed every other warship when she was launched in 1906, starting a naval arms race between Great Britain and Germany.

Queen Victoria
Queen from 1837 to 1901, Victoria was related to almost every European monarch.

Bismarck
With a series of excellent diplomatic and military victories, Otto von Bismarck unified Germany in 1864–1871.

coal mine in the Ruhr valley, Germany

Karl Marx
The communist revolutionary Karl Marx fled Germany and took refuge in London in 1848.

free trade in northern Germany

Revolution
In 1848 the unpopular King Louis-Philippe was overthrown, and France became a republic, a country not governed by a monarch.

a barricade erected in Paris

armaments factory in Pilsen

Napoleon III
The nephew of Napoleon Bonaparte, Louis Napoleon became the president of France in 1848 before seizing power and becoming the emperor in 1851.

French farmers

Emmanuel II
King of Sardinia since 1849, Victor Emmanuel II became the king of a united Italy in 1860.

The unification of Germany
In 1848 Germany consisted of 39 separate states, dominated by Prussia and Austro-Hungary. Otto von Bismarck became the prime minister of Prussia in 1862. He defeated Denmark and Austria, set up a North German Confederation, excluding Austria, and took over Hanover and other German states. In 1871 Prussia defeated France and took its two eastern provinces of Alsace and Lorraine. King Wilhelm I of Prussia was then proclaimed the emperor of Germany (shown above), uniting the remaining 25 German states under Prussian rule.

Gunboat diplomacy
In 1911 Germany sent a gunboat to protect its interests in Morocco, causing a major diplomatic conflict with France.

Atlantic Ocean · North Sea · Mediterranean Sea · NORWAY · OSLO · DENMARK · COPENHAGEN · Schleswig-Holstein · GERMANY · Elbe · Rhine · GREAT BRITAIN · LONDON · NETHERLANDS · BELGIUM · Sedan · Frankfurt · LUXEMBOURG · PARIS · Alsace-Lorraine · SWITZERLAND · Alps · FRANCE · ITALY · ROME · Corsica · Sardinia · Sicily · Pyrenees · PORTUGAL · SPAIN · MADRID · Balearic Islands · MOROCCO

0 500km
0 250 miles

Industrial Revolution
In the second half of the 1800s, Russia industrialized very quickly, opening many new coal mines, steel works, and factories.

DEN
STOCKHOLM

MOSCOW

Trans-continental railroad
The Trans-Siberian Railroad linking Moscow to Vladivostok, on the Pacific coast, was begun in 1891 but not finished until 1916.

Freedom
Serfs (peasants) in Russia received their freedom from their owners in 1861.

Sadowa
In the Seven Weeks' War of 1866, Prussia defeated Austria in Sadowa and ended the country's influence in Germany.

The Dual Monarchy
In 1867 the Austrian empire split into a two-monarch state called "Austro-Hungary." United by its Hapsburg rulers, it had a common army and currency.

RUSSIAN EMPIRE

Ukraine
The Ukraine was the "breadbasket of Russia," as well as its major industrial area.

wheat being harvested in the Ukraine

Potemkin
Revolution broke out in Russia in 1905 and spread to the armed forces. The crew of the Russian battleship *Potemkin* mutinied and fled to Romania.

owa-
niggratz)

VIENNA

AUSTRO-HUNGARIAN EMPIRE

Danube

Odessa

Black Sea

ROMANIA

Ploiesti

BUCHAREST

Romanian oil
Before the development of Middle Eastern oil, most European oil came from the oil wells in Ploïesti.

Bosnia

SERBIA

Balkans

BULGARIA

SOFIA

MONTENEGRO

Constantinople

OTTOMAN EMPIRE

Albania

The Balkan Wars
Two wars in the Balkans in 1912–1913 saw the Ottoman Turks almost expelled from Europe, while Serbia emerged as a major Balkan country.

GREECE

ATHENS

Rhodes

Cyprus

Crete

Garibaldi
In 1859–1860 the Italian nationalist Giuseppe Garibaldi invaded Sicily and Naples with 1,000 troops, and forced them to unify with the rest of Italy.

The Royal Navy
The British Royal Navy commanded the Mediterranean Sea, protecting British sea routes to India.

these dotted lines show the borders between European countries in 1912

Mediterranean Sea

EGYPT

1840–1920

1840

1848 Revolutions in France, Italy, Germany, and Austria against conservative rule
1848 Karl Marx flees to London
1849 Attempts to set up a German National Assembly end in failure

1850

1851 Napoleon III seizes power in France and restores the French Empire

1859–1860 Italian kingdoms united as one country under Victor Emmanuel II

1860

1861 Russian serfs (peasants) are liberated
1862 Bismarck becomes the prime minister of Prussia
1863–1864 Prussia defeats Denmark to gain two northern duchies
1866 Seven Weeks' War
1866 Italy gains Venice from Austria
1867 Creation of North German Confederation under Prussian rule
1867 Creation of Austro-Hungary

1870

1870 Italy takes over the Papal States to complete its unification
1870–1871 Franco-Prussian war ends in French defeat; creation of German Empire
1871 Third Republic is established in France
1878 Romania gains independence from the Ottoman Empire
1878 Great Britain gains Cyprus from Ottomans
1879–1882 Triple Alliance of Germany, Austro-Hungary, and Italy

1880

1883 Death of Karl Marx

1888 Wilhelm II becomes the emperor of Germany

1890

1890 Bismarck resigns

1894 Franco-Russian military alliance

1900

1901 Death of Queen Victoria

1904 Entente Cordiale ("friendly understanding") agreement between Great Britain and France
1906 *HMS Dreadnought* is launched; naval arms race begins in Europe
1908 Austro-Hungary takes over Bosnia
1908 Bulgaria becomes independent

1910

1912–1913 Two Balkan wars redraw the map of southeast Europe
1913 Albania becomes an independent nation
1914 World War I breaks out in Europe

1920

World War I

In the early years of the 1900s, economic, military, and imperial rivalry split Europe in two: Germany and Austro-Hungary (the Central Powers) against Russia, France, and Great Britain (the Allies). The assassination of the heir to the Austro-Hungarian throne was the spark that led to war. Fighting quickly spread around the world as the British and French empires and their allies joined in and attacked Germany's colonies and its allies in Asia and Africa. The war was known as the Great War, because it lasted for four years and involved 65 million soldiers: 8.5 million died, and 21.2 million were injured. Today, this war is called World War I.

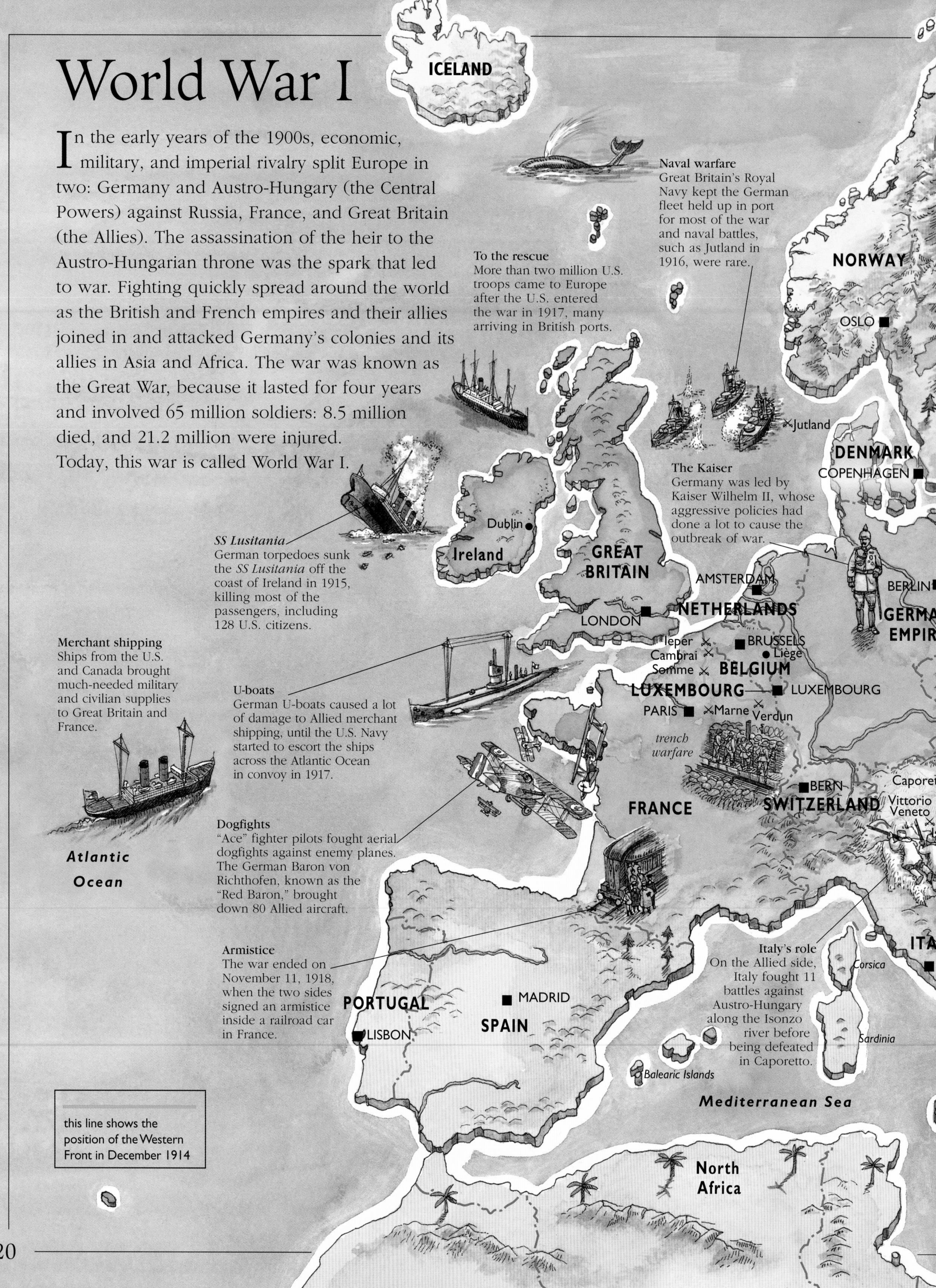
ICELAND
NORWAY
OSLO
Jutland
DENMARK
COPENHAGEN
Dublin
Ireland
GREAT BRITAIN
AMSTERDAM
NETHERLANDS
BERLIN
GERMA
EMPIR
LONDON
Ieper
Cambrai
Somme
BRUSSELS
Liège
BELGIUM
LUXEMBOURG
LUXEMBOURG
PARIS
Marne
Verdun
trench warfare
BERN
SWITZERLAND
Caporet
Vittorio Veneto
FRANCE
Atlantic Ocean
PORTUGAL
LISBON
MADRID
SPAIN
ITA
Corsica
Sardinia
Balearic Islands
Mediterranean Sea
North Africa

Naval warfare
Great Britain's Royal Navy kept the German fleet held up in port for most of the war and naval battles, such as Jutland in 1916, were rare.

To the rescue
More than two million U.S. troops came to Europe after the U.S. entered the war in 1917, many arriving in British ports.

The Kaiser
Germany was led by Kaiser Wilhelm II, whose aggressive policies had done a lot to cause the outbreak of war.

SS Lusitania
German torpedoes sunk the *SS Lusitania* off the coast of Ireland in 1915, killing most of the passengers, including 128 U.S. citizens.

Merchant shipping
Ships from the U.S. and Canada brought much-needed military and civilian supplies to Great Britain and France.

U-boats
German U-boats caused a lot of damage to Allied merchant shipping, until the U.S. Navy started to escort the ships across the Atlantic Ocean in convoy in 1917.

Dogfights
"Ace" fighter pilots fought aerial dogfights against enemy planes. The German Baron von Richthofen, known as the "Red Baron," brought down 80 Allied aircraft.

Armistice
The war ended on November 11, 1918, when the two sides signed an armistice inside a railroad car in France.

Italy's role
On the Allied side, Italy fought 11 battles against Austro-Hungary along the Isonzo river before being defeated in Caporetto.

this line shows the position of the Western Front in December 1914

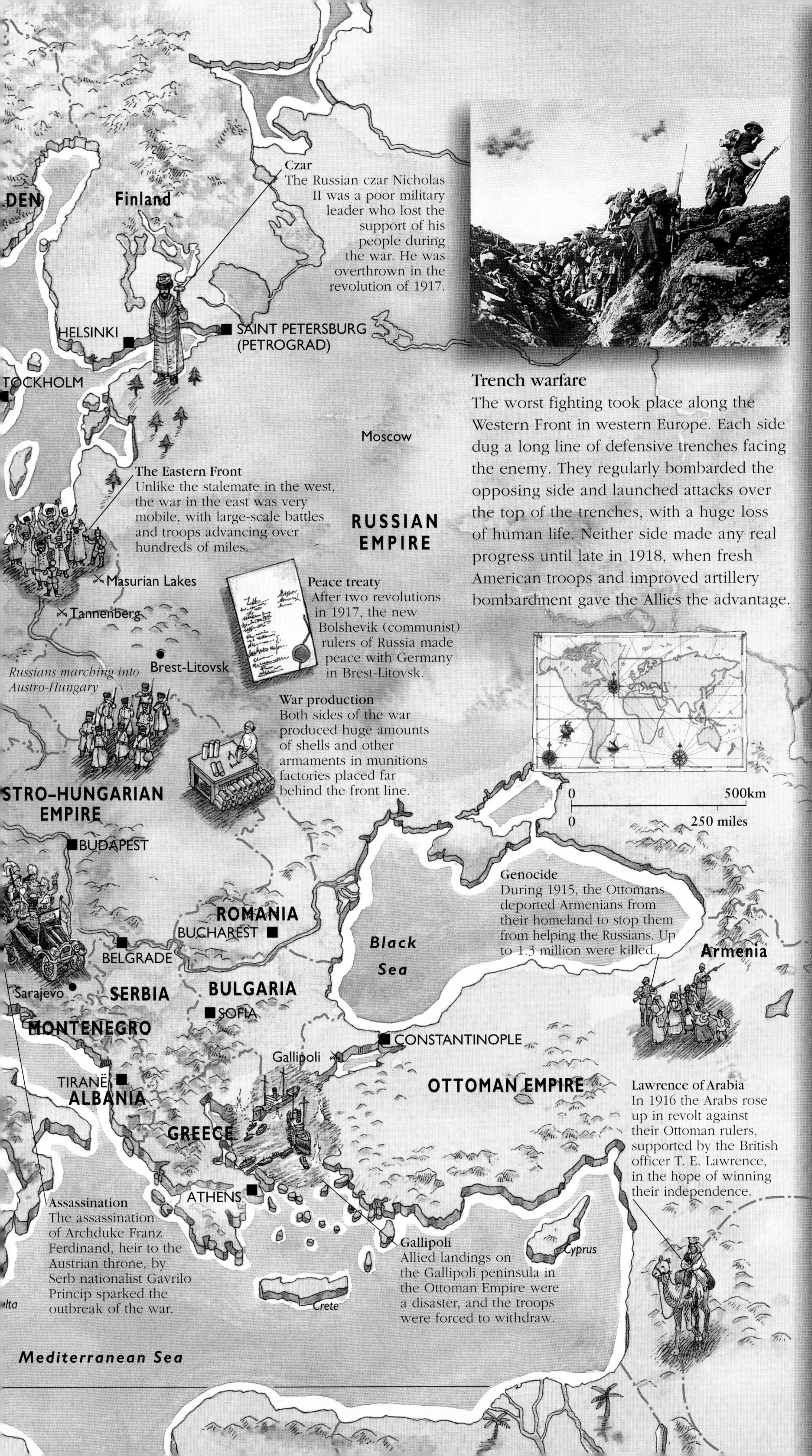

Czar
The Russian czar Nicholas II was a poor military leader who lost the support of his people during the war. He was overthrown in the revolution of 1917.

Trench warfare
The worst fighting took place along the Western Front in western Europe. Each side dug a long line of defensive trenches facing the enemy. They regularly bombarded the opposing side and launched attacks over the top of the trenches, with a huge loss of human life. Neither side made any real progress until late in 1918, when fresh American troops and improved artillery bombardment gave the Allies the advantage.

The Eastern Front
Unlike the stalemate in the west, the war in the east was very mobile, with large-scale battles and troops advancing over hundreds of miles.

Peace treaty
After two revolutions in 1917, the new Bolshevik (communist) rulers of Russia made peace with Germany in Brest-Litovsk.

Russians marching into Austro-Hungary

War production
Both sides of the war produced huge amounts of shells and other armaments in munitions factories placed far behind the front line.

Genocide
During 1915, the Ottomans deported Armenians from their homeland to stop them from helping the Russians. Up to 1.3 million were killed.

Lawrence of Arabia
In 1916 the Arabs rose up in revolt against their Ottoman rulers, supported by the British officer T. E. Lawrence, in the hope of winning their independence.

Assassination
The assassination of Archduke Franz Ferdinand, heir to the Austrian throne, by Serb nationalist Gavrilo Princip sparked the outbreak of the war.

Gallipoli
Allied landings on the Gallipoli peninsula in the Ottoman Empire were a disaster, and the troops were forced to withdraw.

DEN
Finland
HELSINKI
SAINT PETERSBURG (PETROGRAD)
TOCKHOLM
Moscow
RUSSIAN EMPIRE
Masurian Lakes
Tannenberg
Brest-Litovsk
STRO-HUNGARIAN EMPIRE
BUDAPEST
ROMANIA
BUCHAREST
BELGRADE
Sarajevo
SERBIA
BULGARIA
SOFIA
MONTENEGRO
CONSTANTINOPLE
Gallipoli
TIRANË
ALBANIA
OTTOMAN EMPIRE
GREECE
ATHENS
Black Sea
Armenia
Cyprus
Crete
lta
Mediterranean Sea
0 500km
0 250 miles

1914–1919

1914

June, 1914 Archduke Franz Ferdinand is assassinated in Sarajevo; Austro-Hungary declares war on Serbia

Aug., 1914 Germany invades neutral Belgium to attack France; Great Britain, France, and Russia now at war with the Central Powers of Germany and Austro-Hungary

Aug., 1914 Germans defeat the invading Russian army in Tannenberg

Aug., 1914 Allies attack German colonies in Africa, Asia, and the Pacific Ocean

Sept., 1914 Germans advance into France

Oct., 1914 Ottoman Empire enters war on the Central Powers side

Nov., 1914 Trenches built along the length of the Western Front

1915

Feb., 1915 Germans begin submarine blockade of Great Britain

April, 1915 Germans use poison gas on the Western Front for the first time

April, 1915–Jan., 1916 Allied troops seize Gallipoli but fail to capture Constantinople

May, 1915 German torpedoes sink the *SS Lusitania* off the Irish coast

May, 1915 Italy enters the war on the Allied side

May, 1915 Ottoman genocide against Armenians

June, 1915–Aug., 1917 Italy fights 11 battles against Austro-Hungary

Oct., 1915 Central Powers invade Serbia

1916

Jan., 1916 Serbia is defeated

Feb.–Dec., 1916 Germans try but fail to break the French resolve in the Siege of Verdun

May–June, 1916 British Royal Navy wins the Battle of Jutland in the North Sea

June, 1916 Arabs rise up in revolt against their Ottoman rulers

July–Nov., 1916 Massive British losses in the Battle of the Somme

1917

Feb., 1917 Germans begin submarine warfare in the Atlantic Ocean, hitting U.S. shipping

March, 1917 Russian revolution overthrows Czar Nicholas II

April, 1917 U.S. enters the war on the Allied side

July–Nov., 1917 Bloody battle at Ieper (Passchendaele)

Nov.–Dec., 1917 British use massed tanks for the first time in Cambrai, France

Nov., 1917 Bolsheviks seize power in Russia

Dec., 1917 Austro-Hungarians win the Battle of Caporetto against the Italians

1918

March, 1918 Germany and Russia make peace in Brest-Litovsk

March, 1918 Massive German advance into France

July–Aug., 1918 Germans halted at the Second Battle of the Marne, near the Marne river in France

Aug., 1918 Germans pushed back on the Western Front by the Allies

Oct., 1918 Italy defeats Austro-Hungarians in Vittorio Veneto

Oct., 1918 Ottoman Empire makes peace with the Allies

Nov., 1918 German fleet mutinies; Kaiser Wilhelm II abdicates and flees into exile

Nov., 1918 Armistice ends the war

1919

20th-century Russia

In November 1917 one of the major events in world history occured in Russia. The Bolshevik party seized power in a revolution and set up the world's first Communist government. After winning a vicious civil war, the Bolsheviks created a new country in 1922: the Union of Soviet Socialist Republics (U.S.S.R.). Through state control of industry and farming, they turned an agricultural country into an industrial, economic, and military superpower, which sent people into space and had the power to launch nuclear missiles that could destroy entire countries.

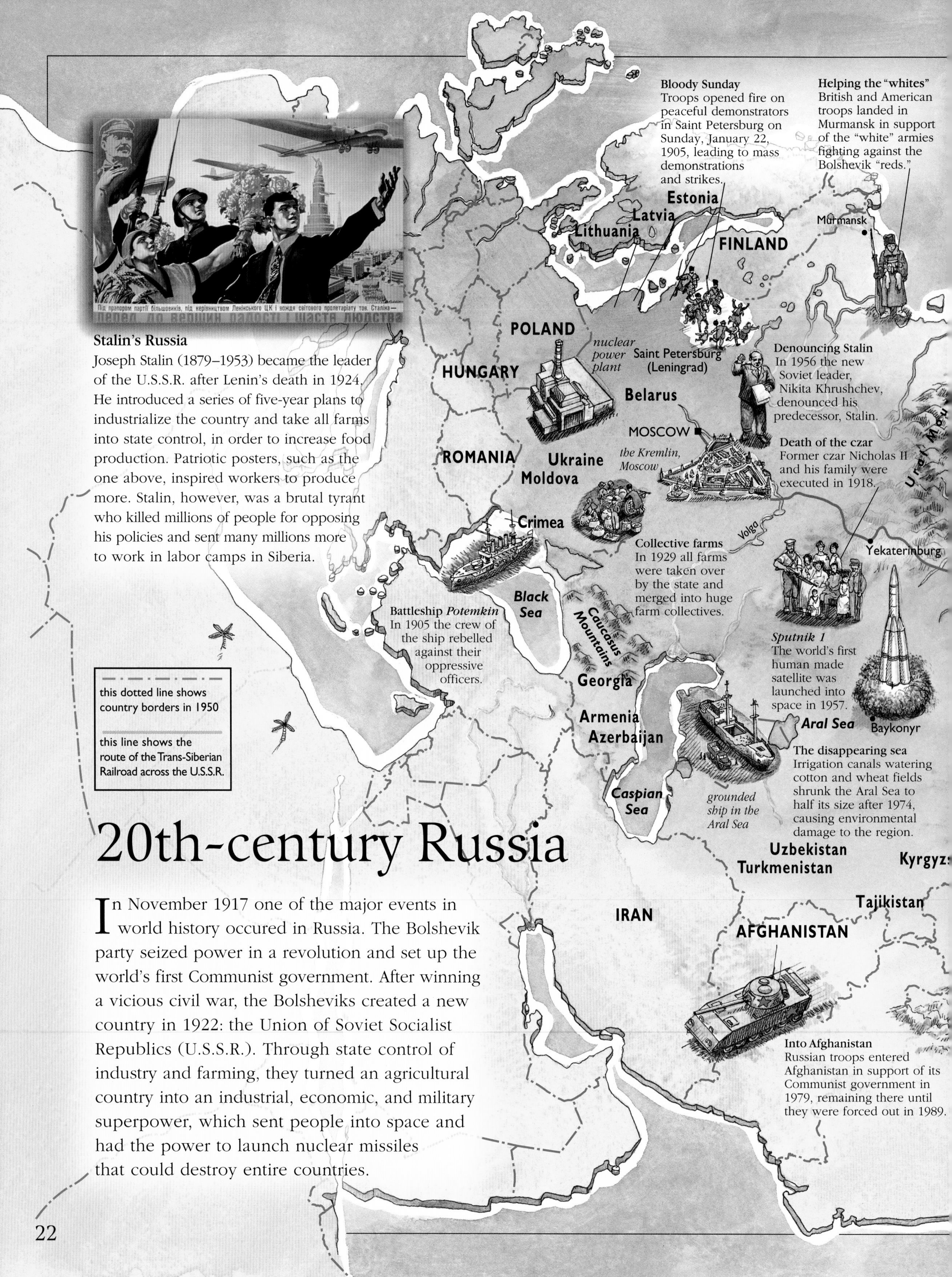

POLAND
HUNGARY
ROMANIA
Ukraine
Moldova
Crimea
Belarus
Estonia
Latvia
Lithuania
FINLAND
Murmansk
Saint Petersburg (Leningrad)
MOSCOW
the Kremlin, Moscow
nuclear power plant
Volga
Yekaterinburg
Ural Mountains
Black Sea
Caucasus Mountains
Georgia
Armenia
Azerbaijan
Caspian Sea
Aral Sea
Baykonyr
grounded ship in the Aral Sea
Uzbekistan
Turkmenistan
Kyrgyz
Tajikistan
IRAN
AFGHANISTAN
this dotted line shows country borders in 1950
this line shows the route of the Trans-Siberian Railroad across the U.S.S.R.

Stalin's Russia
Joseph Stalin (1879–1953) became the leader of the U.S.S.R. after Lenin's death in 1924. He introduced a series of five-year plans to industrialize the country and take all farms into state control, in order to increase food production. Patriotic posters, such as the one above, inspired workers to produce more. Stalin, however, was a brutal tyrant who killed millions of people for opposing his policies and sent many millions more to work in labor camps in Siberia.

Bloody Sunday
Troops opened fire on peaceful demonstrators in Saint Petersburg on Sunday, January 22, 1905, leading to mass demonstrations and strikes.

Helping the "whites"
British and American troops landed in Murmansk in support of the "white" armies fighting against the Bolshevik "reds."

Denouncing Stalin
In 1956 the new Soviet leader, Nikita Khrushchev, denounced his predecessor, Stalin.

Death of the czar
Former czar Nicholas II and his family were executed in 1918.

Collective farms
In 1929 all farms were taken over by the state and merged into huge farm collectives.

Battleship *Potemkin*
In 1905 the crew of the ship rebelled against their oppressive officers.

Sputnik 1
The world's first human made satellite was launched into space in 1957.

The disappearing sea
Irrigation canals watering cotton and wheat fields shrunk the Aral Sea to half its size after 1974, causing environmental damage to the region.

Into Afghanistan
Russian troops entered Afghanistan in support of its Communist government in 1979, remaining there until they were forced out in 1989.

U.S.S.R.
Siberia
Ob
zakhstan
Lake Baikal
MONGOLIA
CHINA
Vladivostok
KOREA
0
1,000km
0
500 miles

Industrial growth
After 1925, major new towns were built close to the Ural Mountains to exploit the region's huge reserves of coal and iron ore.

The "Gulag"
Stalin sent millions of Russians, including criminals and opponents of the government, to the "Gulag"—"corrective labor camps" in the far north and east of the country.

Changing leaders
These traditional Russian *matrioshka* stacking dolls have been updated to show the changing leadership of the U.S.S.R.

Promoting the Revolution
Posters of Lenin and other Bolshevik leaders were used to promote the Bolshevik cause after 1917.

The Red Flag
The Communist red flag, with the hammer and sickle logo, was flown everywhere in the Soviet Union (U.S.S.R.).

Cross-country
The 5,773-mi. Trans-Siberian Railroad, from Moscow in the west to Vladivostok in the east, was finished in 1916.

Japanese Siberia
Japanese troops entered Siberia in 1918 in support of the "whites." They declared an independent republic before they were forced to retreat in 1922.

The "virgin lands" campaign
Khrushchev tried to turn the steppes of Kazakhstan into rolling wheat fields, but overfarming led to soil erosion and poor harvests.

Missile sites
Missile bases were built throughout Siberia, from which the U.S.S.R. could have launched nuclear ICBM—intercontinental ballistic missiles—against its enemy, the U.S.

Tsushima Straits
The Russian Baltic fleet sailed halfway around the world to attack Japan, but it was heavily defeated in the Tsushima Straits in 1905. This forced Russia to make peace with Japan.

1900–1990

1900

1904–1905 Russia is heavily defeated by Japan and loses land in the east
1905 Revolution breaks out across Russia

1910

1914 Russia enters World War I against Germany and Austro-Hungary
1917 Czar Nicholas II abdicates in March
1917 Bolsheviks seize power in November
1918 Treaty of Brest-Litovsk ends war for Russia
1918–1921 Civil war between "reds" and "whites"; western troops help "whites"
1918 Bolsheviks murder Nicholas II and his family

1920

1920–1922 Peasant revolts occur across Russia
1921 "New economic policy" reintroduces free trade to encourage food production
1922 Union of Soviet Socialist Republics (U.S.S.R.) is set up
1924 Death of Lenin; Stalin takes over as leader
1928 First "five-year plan" is introduced to industrialize the country
1929 Collectivization of farms begins

1930

1932–1933 Massive famine in the Ukraine and central Asia as a result of collectivization
1934 Stalin begins show trials and "purges" to get rid of opponents
1938 Stalin's purges at their worst
1939 Nazi-Soviet Pact with Adolf Hitler

1940

1941 Germany invades the U.S.S.R. during World War II
1945 Soviet troops enter Berlin at the end of World War II
1949 U.S.S.R. explodes its first atomic bomb

1950

1953 Death of Stalin; Khrushchev takes over as leader
1954 "Virgin lands" policy is launched to grow more crops
1956 Khrushchev denounces (fiercely criticizes) Stalin in a secret speech
1957 U.S.S.R. launches *Sputnik 1*, the world's first human-made satellite, into space

1960

1961 Soviet cosmonaut Yuri Gagarin becomes the first person in space
1964 Khrushchev is ousted; Leonid Brezhnev takes over as leader

1970

1972 U.S. president Nixon visits the U.S.S.R.
1979 Russian troops enter Afghanistan

1980

1982 Death of Brezhnev; Yuri Andropov and then Konstantin Chernenko succeed him
1985 Mikhail Gorbachev becomes the leader of the U.S.S.R. and begins reforms

1990

The U.S. and the Great Depression:

Economic boom and bust

The U.S. economic boom of the 1920s ended when the New York Stock Exchange crashed in October 1929. As prices and profits collapsed and banks failed, the U.S.—and then the rest of the world—entered a decade-long economic slump. Millions of people lost their jobs or had their incomes reduced, while world trade was cut by almost two thirds between 1929 and 1932. In the U.S., President Roosevelt's New Deal tried to tackle the problem, but it was the threat of war in Europe and Asia and the need to make more weapons that finally produced the jobs that got unemployed people back into work.

The postwar boom
The 1920s was a period of great optimism in America. The economy was booming after World War I, the country was peaceful and prosperous, and women had more freedom than ever before. New forms of entertainment, such as the movies and jazz music, transformed the lives of ordinary people. The picture above shows fashionable women from the 1920s, known as flappers, who summed up the spirit of the decade. Many thought that the boom would last forever.

Hollywood
The invention of a working sound movie system in 1927 transformed the cinema, killing off silent films by 1930. Millions of people flocked to the cinema during the 1930s to see spectacular films, such as *The Wizard of Oz* (below), to take their minds off the economic gloom of their daily lives.

CRUSADE

Worldwide slump
The economic slump began in the U.S., but it had spread around the world by 1931. As millions lost their jobs, social and political unrest grew. In Great Britain, in 1936, 200 unemployed shipyard workers from Jarrow in northeast England marched south to London to draw attention to the poverty and lack of jobs in their town.

The New Deal

In 1933 Franklin D. Roosevelt, pictured here (right), became the U.S. president, pledging "a new deal for the American people." He reformed the banking system, gave financial support to farmers and home owners, and, through the Public Works Administration, set millions of people to work building dams, roads, bridges, schools, and other public projects.

CBS
NBC
NBC

Extreme poverty

Unemployment in the U.S. rose from two million industrial workers in 1928 to 11.6 million in 1932 and stayed high for the rest of the decade. Millions of people lost their life savings when their banks failed. They were forced to rely on soup kitchens (below) and money from the government to keep them alive. From 1934–1938, extreme poverty spread to the farming communities of Oklahoma, Kansas, and other Midwestern states when high winds stripped a huge area of land of its soil.

Europe between the world wars

The years after World War I were chaotic across all of Europe. Germany tried to recover from its defeat in the war. Meanwhile new countries, which had emerged from the former defeated empires, struggled to establish themselves as independent states. Economic chaos after the slump of 1931 only made matters worse, as millions of people lost their jobs. Fascist (extreme right-wing and dictatorial) parties came to power in Italy, most of eastern Europe, and, in 1933, Germany. This divided the continent between democracies, dictatorships, and the U.S.S.R., which was a dictatorship as well as the world's only communist state.

Free Ireland
After hundreds of years of British rule, most of Ireland became an independent country in 1921.

Television
The first regular TV broadcasts in Europe were made by the British Broadcasting Corporation (BBC) in 1936.

Hyper inflation
German economic collapse in 1923 caused such massive inflation that trillions of German marks were needed just to buy simple groceries.

Jews fleeing from the Nazis

"Peace in our time"
In 1938 the British prime minister, Neville Chamberlain, returned from Germany believing that he had reached a peace settlement with Hitler.

Versailles
The leaders of the four victorious Allied powers met in Versailles, outside of Paris, France, to agree to a peace settlement with Germany after World War I.

Nuremberg Rally

Guernica
In April 1937 German bombers destroyed the ancient Basque capital during the Spanish Civil War.

Unemployed
The huge rise in unemployment, after the 1931 worldwide economic slump, led to massive social unrest.

Two dictators
Hitler and Mussolini agreed an alliance—the Rome-Berlin Axis—in 1936. Other countries joined the axis during World War II.

Civil war
Almost one million people lost their lives during the Spanish Civil War.

NORW
OSL
North Sea
DENM
GREAT BRITAIN
DUBLIN
IRISH FREE STATE
AMSTERDAM
NETHERLANDS
LONDON
Rhine
BRUSSELS
BELGIUM
Rhineland
PARIS
Atlantic Ocean
SWITZERLAND
BERN
FRANCE
Guernica
Basque Country
SPAIN
PORTUGAL
MADRID
LISBON
Sardinia
Balearic Islands
Mediterranean Sea

The Spanish Civil War
In 1936 the Spanish army, led by the Nationalist General Francisco Franco, rose up in revolt against the democratic Republican government. The civil war that followed lasted three years and involved several international forces: the U.S.S.R. sent arms to the Republicans, Germany and Italy sent troops and planes to the Nationalist rebels, volunteers from around the world fought on both sides, while Great Britain and France remained neutral. The war ended with a Nationalist victory in 1939, starting 36 years of authoritarian government in Spain.

FINLAND
HELSINKI
WEDEN
TOCKHOLM
TALLINN
ESTONIA
RIGA
LATVIA
LITHUANIA
NHAGEN
East Prussia
GDAŃSK (DANZIG)
The U.S.S.R.
As the world's only Communist state, the U.S.S.R. under Stalin mostly stayed out of European politics. It watched the rise of Hitler with alarm, before allying with him in 1939.
MOSCOW
U . S . S . R .
The Polish Corridor
The thin strip of land giving Poland access to the Baltic Sea contained many Germans and was a source of tension between the two countries.
ERLIN
WARSAW
RMANY
Starvation
Under Joseph Stalin, millions of peasants starved as their farms were taken under state control.
Communist Hungary
The Communists under Béla Kun seized power in Hungary in 1919 but were quickly forced out by an invading Romanian army.
detenland
GUE
POLAND
CZECHOSLOVAKIA
VIENNA
Union
In March 1938 Germany occupied Austria, causing the *Anschluss*—the union of both countries.
BUDAPEST
HUNGARY
TRIA
German troops in Austria
ROMANIA
BUCHAREST
Danube
Black Sea
BELGRADE
YUGOSLAVIA
BULGARIA
SOFIA
LY
OME
TIRANË
ALBANIA
TURKEY
Atatürk
Kemal Atatürk, a World War I hero, abolished the Turkish sultanate in 1922 and set up an independent republic in 1923.
Greek immigration
More than one million Greeks were forced to flee from Asia Minor when Turkey occupied some Greek cities in 1922.
GREECE
ATHENS
Cyprus
Sicily
Crete
Yugoslavia
Yugoslavia became one country in 1919, merging the Serb, Croat, and Slovene peoples into one state.
Mussolini
Mussolini and his Fascist Party took over power in Italy in 1922 and soon crushed any opposition to their rule.
Mediterranean Sea
0 500km
0 250 miles

1910–1940

1910

1918 World War I ends with the defeat of Germany and Austro-Hungary
1919–1920 Treaty of Versailles, and other peace treaties, are signed in France to draw up the postwar borders of Europe

1919 Yugoslavia, Hungary, Czechoslovakia, Poland, Finland, and three Baltic states (Estonia, Latvia, and Lithuania) emerge from the ruins of the Austro-Hungarian and Russian empires

1920

1920 Communists try to take power in Germany
1920–1921 Poland wins war against the U.S.S.R.
1921 Irish Free State is established within the British Empire

1922 Mussolini takes power in Italy
1922 Greeks expelled from Asia Minor
1922 Germany and the U.S.S.R. sign an economic treaty

1923 Turkish republic is set up under Kemal Atatürk

1926 General Strike in Great Britain

1928 Kellogg-Briand Pact is signed in Paris: all countries agree to renounce war

1929 Beginning of the Great Depression

1930

1931 Worldwide economic slump
1931 Spain becomes a republic

1933 Adolf Hitler comes to power in Germany
1934 Greece, Romania, Turkey, and Yugoslavia sign the Balkan Pact against Germany and the U.S.S.R.
1935–1936 Italy invades Abyssinia (Ethiopia)
1936 British Broadcasting Corporation (BBC) begins regular TV broadcasts
1936 Germany reoccupies the demilitarized Rhineland
1936 Germany and Italy agree the Rome-Berlin Axis alliance
1936–1939 Spanish Civil War

1938 Germany takes over Austria
1938 Germany takes Sudetenland from Czechoslovakia after Great Britain, France, and Italy agree to terms with Germany in Munich
1939 Germany takes over the rest of Czechoslovakia
1939 Italy occupies Albania
1939 Nazi-Soviet pact: Germany and Russia agree to partition (split up) Poland
1939 Germany invades Poland, beginning World War II

1940

The war in Europe

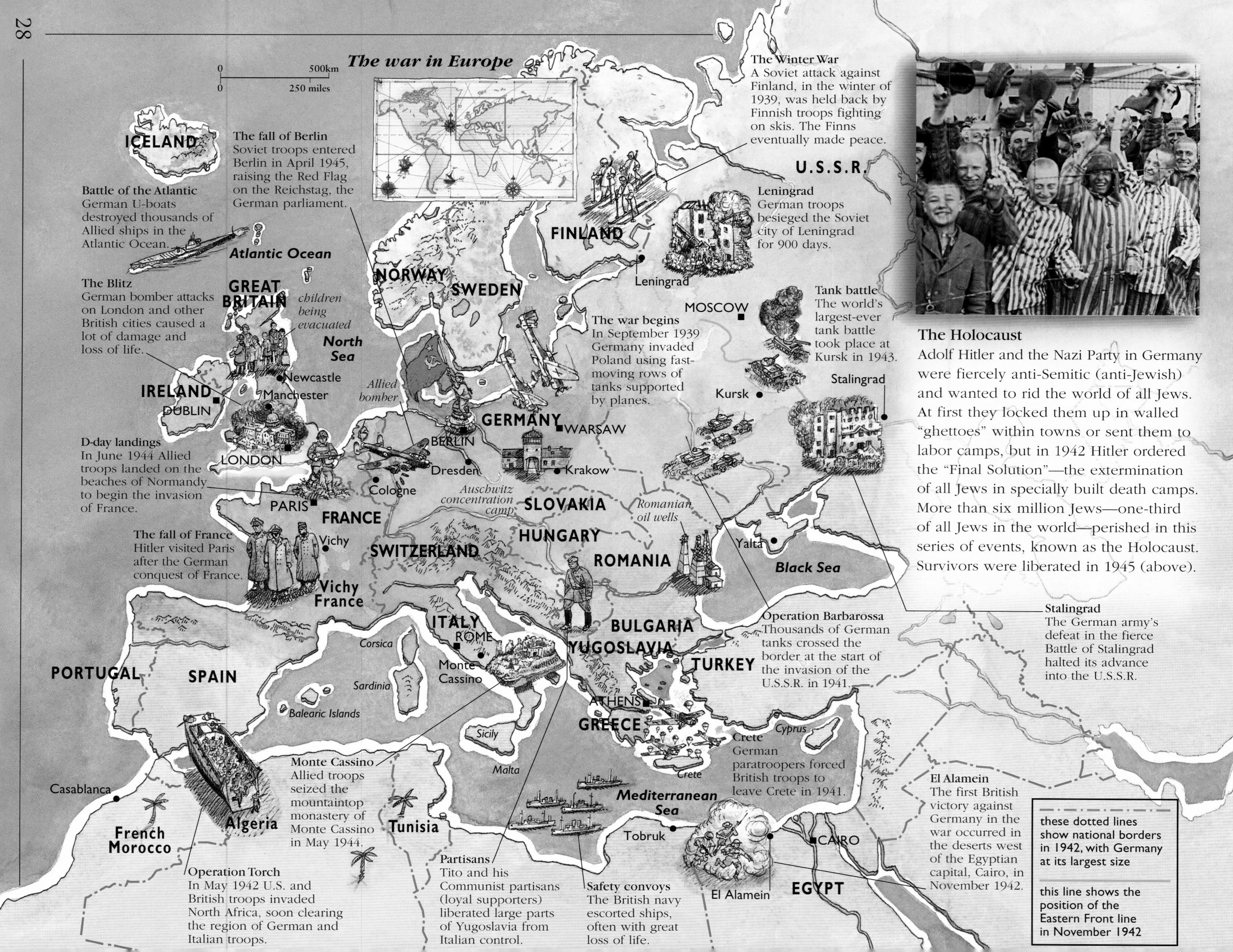
0 500km
0 250 miles
ICELAND
Atlantic Ocean
GREAT BRITAIN
children being evacuated
North Sea
Newcastle
Manchester
IRELAND
DUBLIN
LONDON
PARIS
FRANCE
Vichy
Vichy France
NORWAY
SWEDEN
FINLAND
Leningrad
U.S.S.R.
MOSCOW
Kursk
Stalingrad
Allied bomber
Cologne
BERLIN
Dresden
GERMANY
WARSAW
Krakow
Auschwitz concentration camp
SLOVAKIA
HUNGARY
SWITZERLAND
Romanian oil wells
ROMANIA
Yalta
Black Sea
BULGARIA
YUGOSLAVIA
TURKEY
ITALY
ROME
Monte Cassino
Corsica
Sardinia
Balearic Islands
Sicily
Malta
PORTUGAL
SPAIN
ATHENS
GREECE
Cyprus
Crete
Mediterranean Sea
Tobruk
CAIRO
El Alamein
EGYPT
Casablanca
French Morocco
Algeria
Tunisia
these dotted lines show national borders in 1942, with Germany at its largest size
this line shows the position of the Eastern Front line in November 1942

Battle of the Atlantic
German U-boats destroyed thousands of Allied ships in the Atlantic Ocean.

The fall of Berlin
Soviet troops entered Berlin in April 1945, raising the Red Flag on the Reichstag, the German parliament.

The Blitz
German bomber attacks on London and other British cities caused a lot of damage and loss of life.

D-day landings
In June 1944 Allied troops landed on the beaches of Normandy to begin the invasion of France.

The fall of France
Hitler visited Paris after the German conquest of France.

The Winter War
A Soviet attack against Finland, in the winter of 1939, was held back by Finnish troops fighting on skis. The Finns eventually made peace.

Leningrad
German troops besieged the Soviet city of Leningrad for 900 days.

The war begins
In September 1939 Germany invaded Poland using fast-moving rows of tanks supported by planes.

Tank battle
The world's largest-ever tank battle took place at Kursk in 1943.

Operation Barbarossa
Thousands of German tanks crossed the border at the start of the invasion of the U.S.S.R. in 1941.

Stalingrad
The German army's defeat in the fierce Battle of Stalingrad halted its advance into the U.S.S.R.

Crete
German paratroopers forced British troops to leave Crete in 1941.

El Alamein
The first British victory against Germany in the war occurred in the deserts west of the Egyptian capital, Cairo, in November 1942.

Monte Cassino
Allied troops seized the mountaintop monastery of Monte Cassino in May 1944.

Operation Torch
In May 1942 U.S. and British troops invaded North Africa, soon clearing the region of German and Italian troops.

Partisans
Tito and his Communist partisans (loyal supporters) liberated large parts of Yugoslavia from Italian control.

Safety convoys
The British navy escorted ships, often with great loss of life.

The Holocaust

Adolf Hitler and the Nazi Party in Germany were fiercely anti-Semitic (anti-Jewish) and wanted to rid the world of all Jews. At first they locked them up in walled "ghettoes" within towns or sent them to labor camps, but in 1942 Hitler ordered the "Final Solution"—the extermination of all Jews in specially built death camps. More than six million Jews—one-third of all Jews in the world—perished in this series of events, known as the Holocaust. Survivors were liberated in 1945 (above).

World War II

The most terrible and expensive war in history broke out in September 1939 when German troops invaded Poland. Great Britain and France declared war on Germany, and within a year, most of Europe was under German occupation. In 1941 the war became global: Germany invaded the U.S.S.R., and Germany's ally, Japan, attacked the U.S. The war was fought on land, at sea, and in the air, with terrible casualties on both sides. At least 55 million people, both military and civilian, lost their lives before Germany and Japan were defeated in 1945. Around 20 million people were killed in the U.S.S.R. alone.

these dotted lines show national borders in December 1941
this line shows the maximum extent of Japanese territory in June 1942
China
The Japanese invaded China in 1937 but failed to conquer much more than the coastal regions of this huge country.
Hiroshima
The U.S. dropped two atomic bombs on Hiroshima and Nagasaki in August 1945, ending the war in the Pacific.
Burma railroad
The Japanese forced Allied prisoners of war to build a railroad from Thailand to Burma.
Iwo Jima
U.S. marines took Iwo Jima from Japan in March 1945.
Midway
A major U.S. victory in Midway, in June 1942, kept the strategic island under U.S. control.
Pearl Harbor
Japanese bombers attacked the U.S. fleet in Hawaii in December 1941, bringing the U.S. into the war.
Kamikaze pilots
Japanese kamikaze ("divine wind") suicide pilots dive-bombed enemy ships.
Okinawa
The capture of Okinawa allowed Allied bombers to destroy the main Japanese cities.
Southeast Asia
Japanese troops overran all of southeast Asia by the spring of 1942, capturing the crucial British base in Singapore.
Australia
The Americans used Australia as a strategic location for military bases. The Japanese bombed their base at Darwin in 1942.
Coral Sea
The first-ever battle between aircraft carriers took place in the Coral Sea in May 1942.
Aleutian Islands
JAPAN
TOKYO
Hiroshima
Nagasaki
CHINA
SHANGHAI
Okinawa
INDIA
Calcutta
BURMA
THAILAND
BANGKOK
Philippines
Singapore
Dutch East Indies
Papua
Port Moresby
Darwin
AUSTRALIA
North Pacific Ocean
South Pacific Ocean
Midway
Midway Islands
Pearl Harbor
Hawaii
Hawaiian Islands
Iwo Jima
Mariana Islands
Caroline Islands
Marshall Islands
Coral Sea
New Hebrides
Fiji Islands
Indian Ocean
0 2,000km
0 1,000 miles

The war in the Pacific

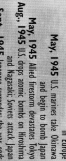

1939–1946

1939

Sept., 1939 Germany invades Poland; Great Britain, and France declare war—start of World War II

Nov., 1939 U.S.S.R. invades Finland

1940

April, 1940 Germany invades Denmark and Norway

May, 1940 Germany invades the Low Countries and France

June, 1940 Italy enters war on Germany's side

July–Oct., 1940 Battle of Britain: the British air force defeats the German Luftwaffe (air force)

Sept., 1940 Blitz against British cities begins

Sept., 1940 Italians invade Egypt

Oct., 1940 Italians invade Greece

Oct., 1940 Hungary, Romania, and Bulgaria join Germany and Italy

1941

April, 1941 Germany invades Yugoslavia and Greece

May, 1941 British are forced out of Crete

June, 1941 Operation Barbarossa: Germany invades the U.S.S.R.

Sept., 1941 Siege of Leningrad begins

Dec., 1941 Japan attacks Pearl Harbor; the U.S. enters the war

Dec., 1941 German advance is stopped outside of Moscow

1942

Jan., 1941 Hitler orders extermination of all Jews

Feb.–March, 1942 Japanese bomb Darwin; Japanese take Malaya, Singapore, and Dutch East Indies

April–May, 1942 Battle of the Coral Sea halts the Japanese advance

May, 1942 Japanese take the Philippines

May, 1942 First British area bombing campaign against Cologne

Oct.–Nov., 1942 British victory in El Alamein

Nov., 1942 Operation Torch: Allied invasion of North Africa

Nov., 1942 Germans occupy Vichy, France

1943

Feb., 1943 Germans surrender in Stalingrad

April, 1943 Jewish uprising in Warsaw, Poland

May, 1943 Battle of the Atlantic ends

May, 1943 German and Italian troops surrender in Tunisia

June–Aug., 1943 Soviets defeat German tanks in Kursk

July, 1943 Allies invade Italy

1944

Jan., 1944 Siege of Leningrad ends

June, 1944 D-day: Allied troops invade France

June, 1944 Allies begin their bombing of southern Japan from Chinese bases

July, 1944 Soviet troops enter Poland

Aug., 1944 Allied troops liberate Paris

Oct., 1944 British troops liberate Greece

Oct., 1944 Battle of Leyte Gulf in the Philippines ends Japanese naval power

Nov., 1944 First Japanese kamikaze attacks on Allied ships

1945

March, 1945 Allied troops cross the Rhine river

March, 1945 U.S. marines take Iwo Jima in the Pacific

April, 1945 Soviet troops enter Berlin

April, 1945 Hitler commits suicide

May, 1945 Italy and Germany surrender: peace in Europe

May, 1945 U.S. marines take Okinawa and begin to bomb Japan

May, 1945 Allied firestorm devastates Tokyo

Aug., 1945 U.S. drops atomic bombs on Hiroshima and Nagasaki; Soviets attack Japan

Sept., 1945 Japanese surrender: the war ends

1946

The Cold War

The U.S. and U.S.S.R. emerged victorious at the end of World War II, but political differences between them soon erupted into a "cold" war—one that never reached an all-out military conflict, despite the ever-present threat of war. By 1949, the world was roughly divided between pro-Western and pro-communist states. Allies of the two sides fought wars on their behalf, such as in Korea and Vietnam, while both the U.S.S.R. and U.S. built up huge arsenals of nuclear and other weapons. Attempts to achieve an understanding between the two sides failed in the 1970s. By the late 1980s, the U.S. had outspent the U.S.S.R. and forced it toward financial ruin. The collapse of communism brought the Cold War to an end in 1991.

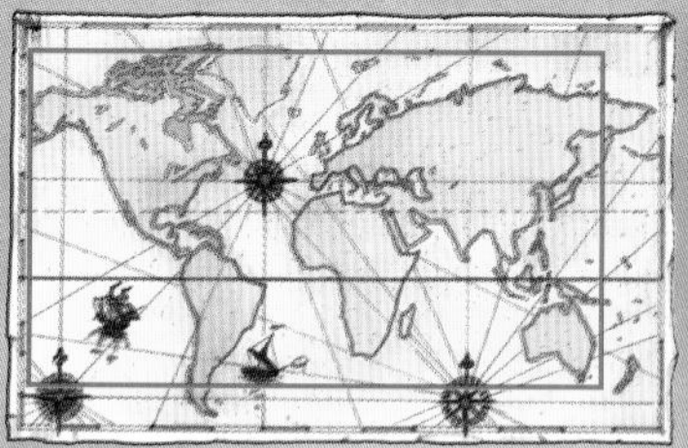

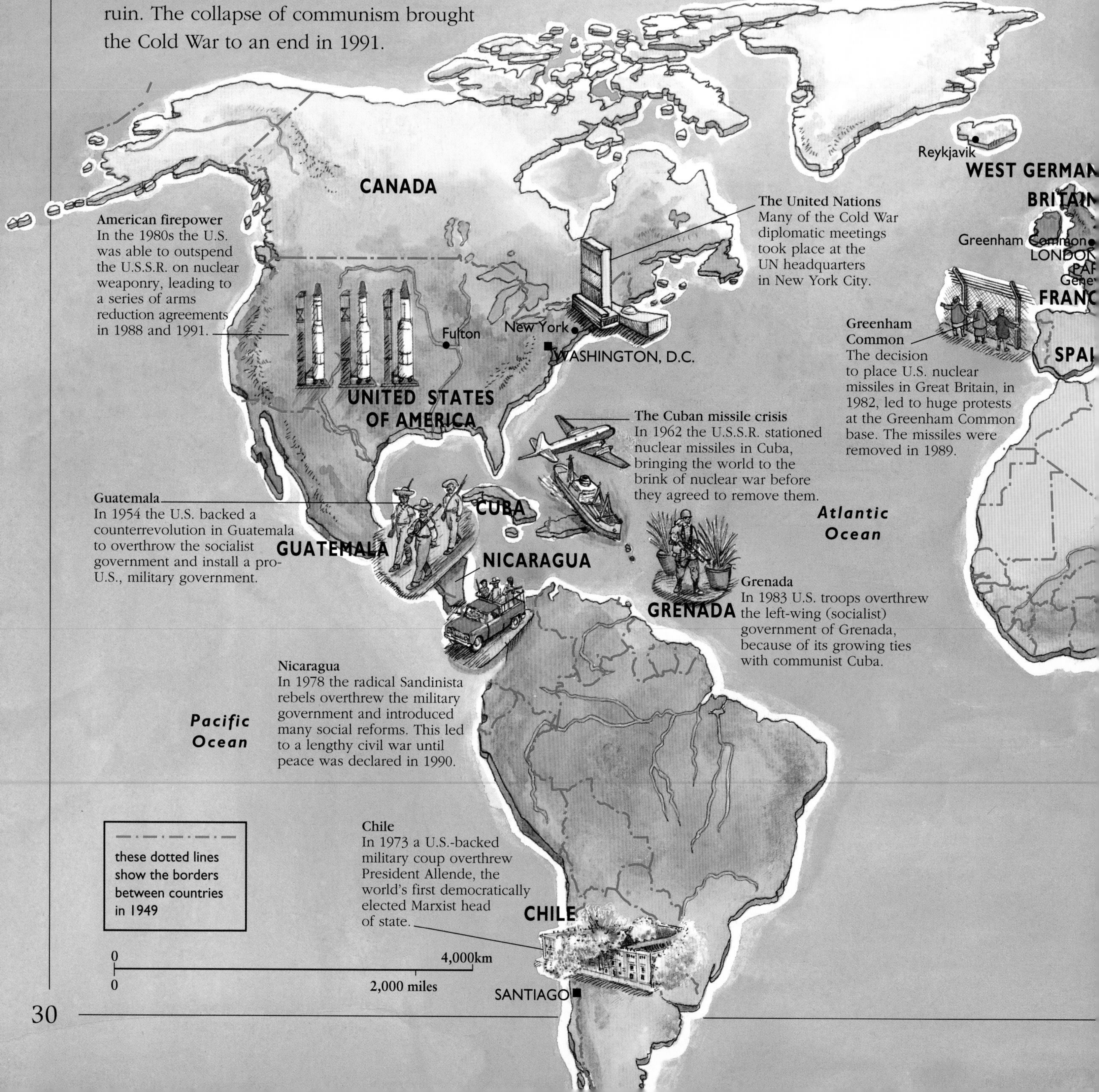

American firepower
In the 1980s the U.S. was able to outspend the U.S.S.R. on nuclear weaponry, leading to a series of arms reduction agreements in 1988 and 1991.

The United Nations
Many of the Cold War diplomatic meetings took place at the UN headquarters in New York City.

Greenham Common
The decision to place U.S. nuclear missiles in Great Britain, in 1982, led to huge protests at the Greenham Common base. The missiles were removed in 1989.

The Cuban missile crisis
In 1962 the U.S.S.R. stationed nuclear missiles in Cuba, bringing the world to the brink of nuclear war before they agreed to remove them.

Guatemala
In 1954 the U.S. backed a counterrevolution in Guatemala to overthrow the socialist government and install a pro-U.S., military government.

Grenada
In 1983 U.S. troops overthrew the left-wing (socialist) government of Grenada, because of its growing ties with communist Cuba.

Nicaragua
In 1978 the radical Sandinista rebels overthrew the military government and introduced many social reforms. This led to a lengthy civil war until peace was declared in 1990.

Chile
In 1973 a U.S.-backed military coup overthrew President Allende, the world's first democratically elected Marxist head of state.

these dotted lines show the borders between countries in 1949

0 — 4,000km
0 — 2,000 miles

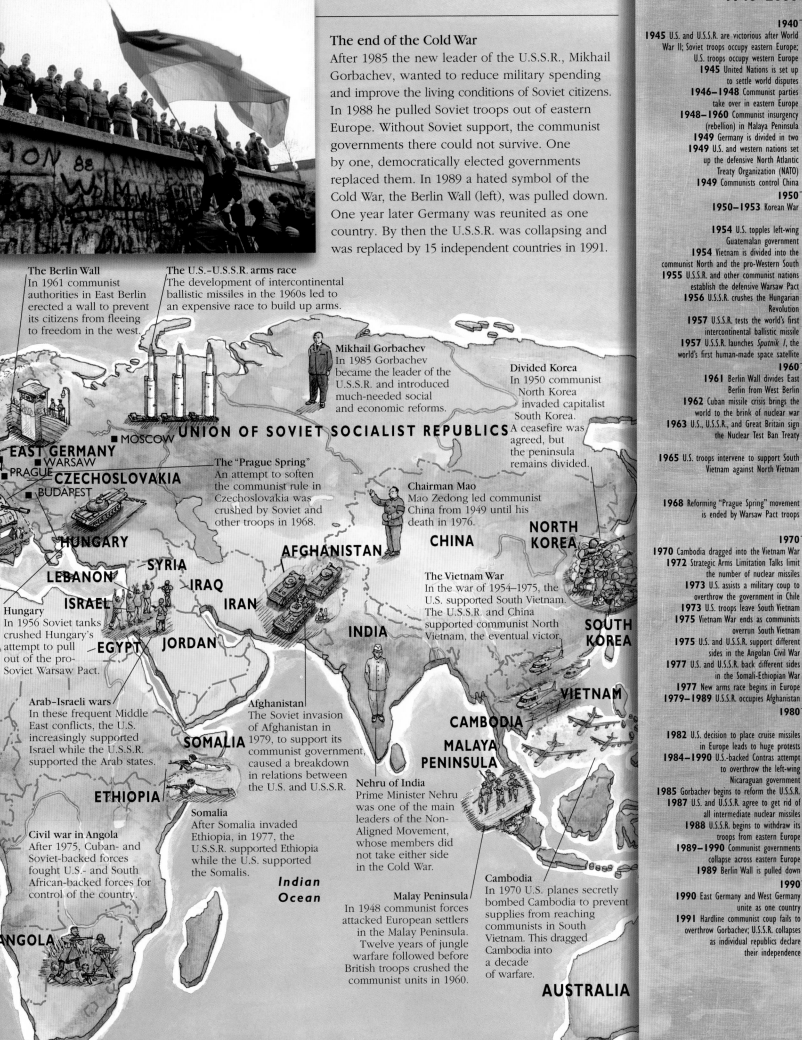

The end of the Cold War

After 1985 the new leader of the U.S.S.R., Mikhail Gorbachev, wanted to reduce military spending and improve the living conditions of Soviet citizens. In 1988 he pulled Soviet troops out of eastern Europe. Without Soviet support, the communist governments there could not survive. One by one, democratically elected governments replaced them. In 1989 a hated symbol of the Cold War, the Berlin Wall (left), was pulled down. One year later Germany was reunited as one country. By then the U.S.S.R. was collapsing and was replaced by 15 independent countries in 1991.

UNION OF SOVIET SOCIALIST REPUBLICS
MOSCOW
EAST GERMANY
WARSAW
PRAGUE
CZECHOSLOVAKIA
BUDAPEST
HUNGARY
SYRIA
LEBANON
IRAQ
ISRAEL
IRAN
EGYPT
JORDAN
AFGHANISTAN
CHINA
NORTH KOREA
SOUTH KOREA
INDIA
VIETNAM
CAMBODIA
MALAYA PENINSULA
SOMALIA
ETHIOPIA
ANGOLA
Indian Ocean
AUSTRALIA

The Berlin Wall
In 1961 communist authorities in East Berlin erected a wall to prevent its citizens from fleeing to freedom in the west.

The U.S.-U.S.S.R. arms race
The development of intercontinental ballistic missiles in the 1960s led to an expensive race to build up arms.

Mikhail Gorbachev
In 1985 Gorbachev became the leader of the U.S.S.R. and introduced much-needed social and economic reforms.

Divided Korea
In 1950 communist North Korea invaded capitalist South Korea. A ceasefire was agreed, but the peninsula remains divided.

The "Prague Spring"
An attempt to soften the communist rule in Czechoslovakia was crushed by Soviet and other troops in 1968.

Chairman Mao
Mao Zedong led communist China from 1949 until his death in 1976.

The Vietnam War
In the war of 1954–1975, the U.S. supported South Vietnam. The U.S.S.R. and China supported communist North Vietnam, the eventual victor.

Hungary
In 1956 Soviet tanks crushed Hungary's attempt to pull out of the pro-Soviet Warsaw Pact.

Arab-Israeli wars
In these frequent Middle East conflicts, the U.S. increasingly supported Israel while the U.S.S.R. supported the Arab states.

Afghanistan
The Soviet invasion of Afghanistan in 1979, to support its communist government, caused a breakdown in relations between the U.S. and U.S.S.R.

Nehru of India
Prime Minister Nehru was one of the main leaders of the Non-Aligned Movement, whose members did not take either side in the Cold War.

Somalia
After Somalia invaded Ethiopia, in 1977, the U.S.S.R. supported Ethiopia while the U.S. supported the Somalis.

Civil war in Angola
After 1975, Cuban- and Soviet-backed forces fought U.S.- and South African-backed forces for control of the country.

Malay Peninsula
In 1948 communist forces attacked European settlers in the Malay Peninsula. Twelve years of jungle warfare followed before British troops crushed the communist units in 1960.

Cambodia
In 1970 U.S. planes secretly bombed Cambodia to prevent supplies from reaching communists in South Vietnam. This dragged Cambodia into a decade of warfare.

1940–2000

1940

1945 U.S. and U.S.S.R. are victorious after World War II; Soviet troops occupy eastern Europe; U.S. troops occupy western Europe
1945 United Nations is set up to settle world disputes
1946–1948 Communist parties take over in eastern Europe
1948–1960 Communist insurgency (rebellion) in Malaya Peninsula
1949 Germany is divided in two
1949 U.S. and western nations set up the defensive North Atlantic Treaty Organization (NATO)
1949 Communists control China

1950

1950–1953 Korean War
1954 U.S. topples left-wing Guatemalan government
1954 Vietnam is divided into the communist North and the pro-Western South
1955 U.S.S.R. and other communist nations establish the defensive Warsaw Pact
1956 U.S.S.R. crushes the Hungarian Revolution
1957 U.S.S.R. tests the world's first intercontinental ballistic missile
1957 U.S.S.R. launches *Sputnik 1*, the world's first human-made space satellite

1960

1961 Berlin Wall divides East Berlin from West Berlin
1962 Cuban missile crisis brings the world to the brink of nuclear war
1963 U.S., U.S.S.R., and Great Britain sign the Nuclear Test Ban Treaty
1965 U.S. troops intervene to support South Vietnam against North Vietnam
1968 Reforming "Prague Spring" movement is ended by Warsaw Pact troops

1970

1970 Cambodia dragged into the Vietnam War
1972 Strategic Arms Limitation Talks limit the number of nuclear missiles
1973 U.S. assists a military coup to overthrow the government in Chile
1973 U.S. troops leave South Vietnam
1975 Vietnam War ends as communists overrun South Vietnam
1975 U.S. and U.S.S.R. support different sides in the Angolan Civil War
1977 U.S. and U.S.S.R. back different sides in the Somali-Ethiopian War
1977 New arms race begins in Europe
1979–1989 U.S.S.R. occupies Afghanistan

1980

1982 U.S. decision to place cruise missiles in Europe leads to huge protests
1984–1990 U.S.-backed Contras attempt to overthrow the left-wing Nicaraguan government
1985 Gorbachev begins to reform the U.S.S.R.
1987 U.S. and U.S.S.R. agree to get rid of all intermediate nuclear missiles
1988 U.S.S.R. begins to withdraw its troops from eastern Europe
1989–1990 Communist governments collapse across eastern Europe
1989 Berlin Wall is pulled down

1990

1990 East Germany and West Germany unite as one country
1991 Hardline communist coup fails to overthrow Gorbachev; U.S.S.R. collapses as individual republics declare their independence

2000

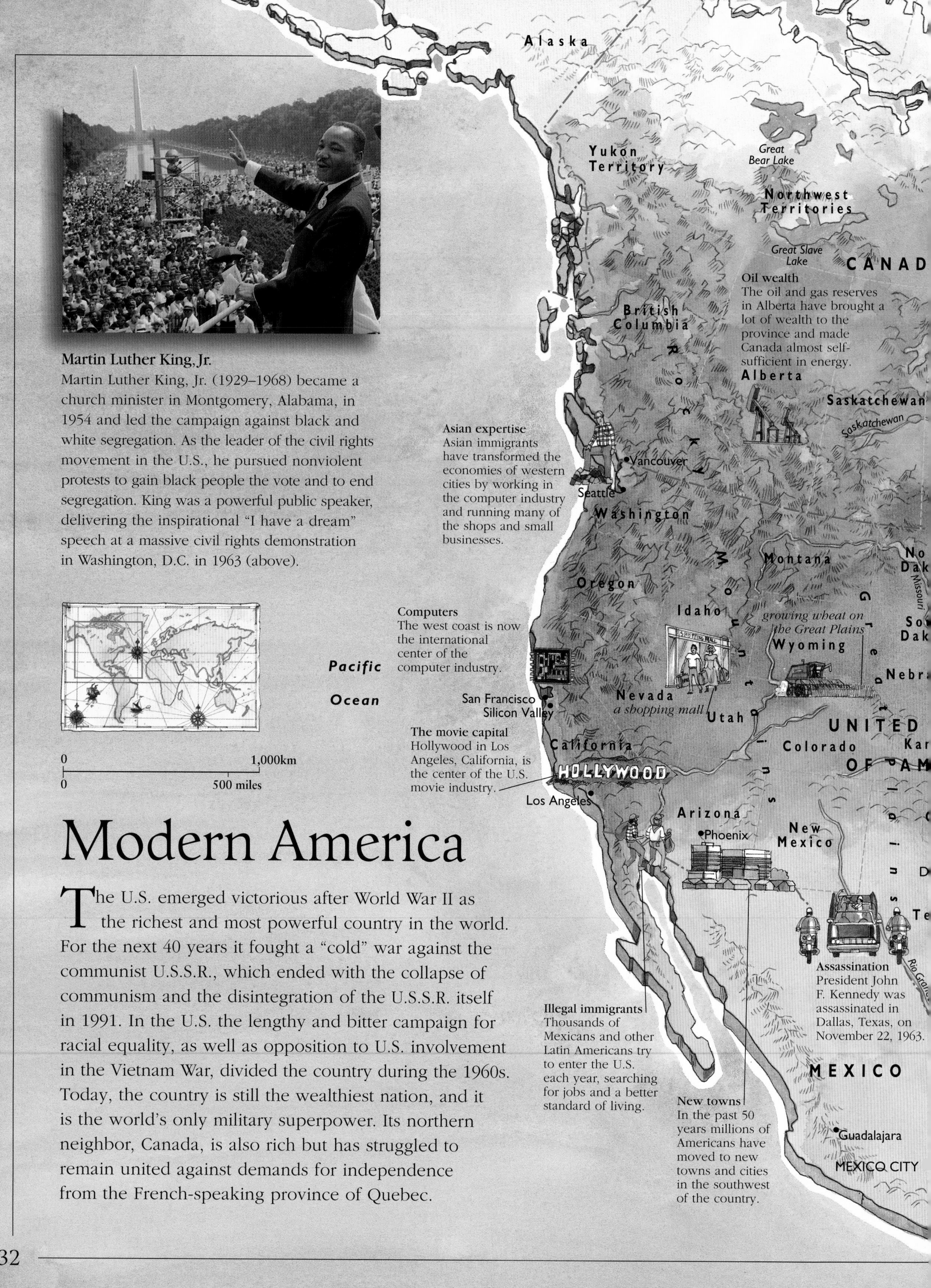
Alaska
Yukon Territory
Great Bear Lake
Northwest Territories
Great Slave Lake
CANAD
Oil wealth
The oil and gas reserves in Alberta have brought a lot of wealth to the province and made Canada almost self-sufficient in energy.
British Columbia
Alberta
Saskatchewan
Saskatchewan
Asian expertise
Asian immigrants have transformed the economies of western cities by working in the computer industry and running many of the shops and small businesses.
Vancouver
Seattle
Washington
Montana
Oregon
Idaho
Computers
The west coast is now the international center of the computer industry.
growing wheat on the Great Plains
Wyoming
Pacific
Ocean
San Francisco
Silicon Valley
Nevada
a shopping mall
Utah
The movie capital
Hollywood in Los Angeles, California, is the center of the U.S. movie industry.
California
HOLLYWOOD
Colorado
UNITED
Los Angeles
Arizona
Phoenix
New Mexico
Assassination
President John F. Kennedy was assassinated in Dallas, Texas, on November 22, 1963.
Illegal immigrants
Thousands of Mexicans and other Latin Americans try to enter the U.S. each year, searching for jobs and a better standard of living.
MEXICO
New towns
In the past 50 years millions of Americans have moved to new towns and cities in the southwest of the country.
Guadalajara
MEXICO CITY
0 1,000km
0 500 miles

Martin Luther King, Jr.
Martin Luther King, Jr. (1929–1968) became a church minister in Montgomery, Alabama, in 1954 and led the campaign against black and white segregation. As the leader of the civil rights movement in the U.S., he pursued nonviolent protests to gain black people the vote and to end segregation. King was a powerful public speaker, delivering the inspirational "I have a dream" speech at a massive civil rights demonstration in Washington, D.C. in 1963 (above).

Modern America

The U.S. emerged victorious after World War II as the richest and most powerful country in the world. For the next 40 years it fought a "cold" war against the communist U.S.S.R., which ended with the collapse of communism and the disintegration of the U.S.S.R. itself in 1991. In the U.S. the lengthy and bitter campaign for racial equality, as well as opposition to U.S. involvement in the Vietnam War, divided the country during the 1960s. Today, the country is still the wealthiest nation, and it is the world's only military superpower. Its northern neighbor, Canada, is also rich but has struggled to remain united against demands for independence from the French-speaking province of Quebec.

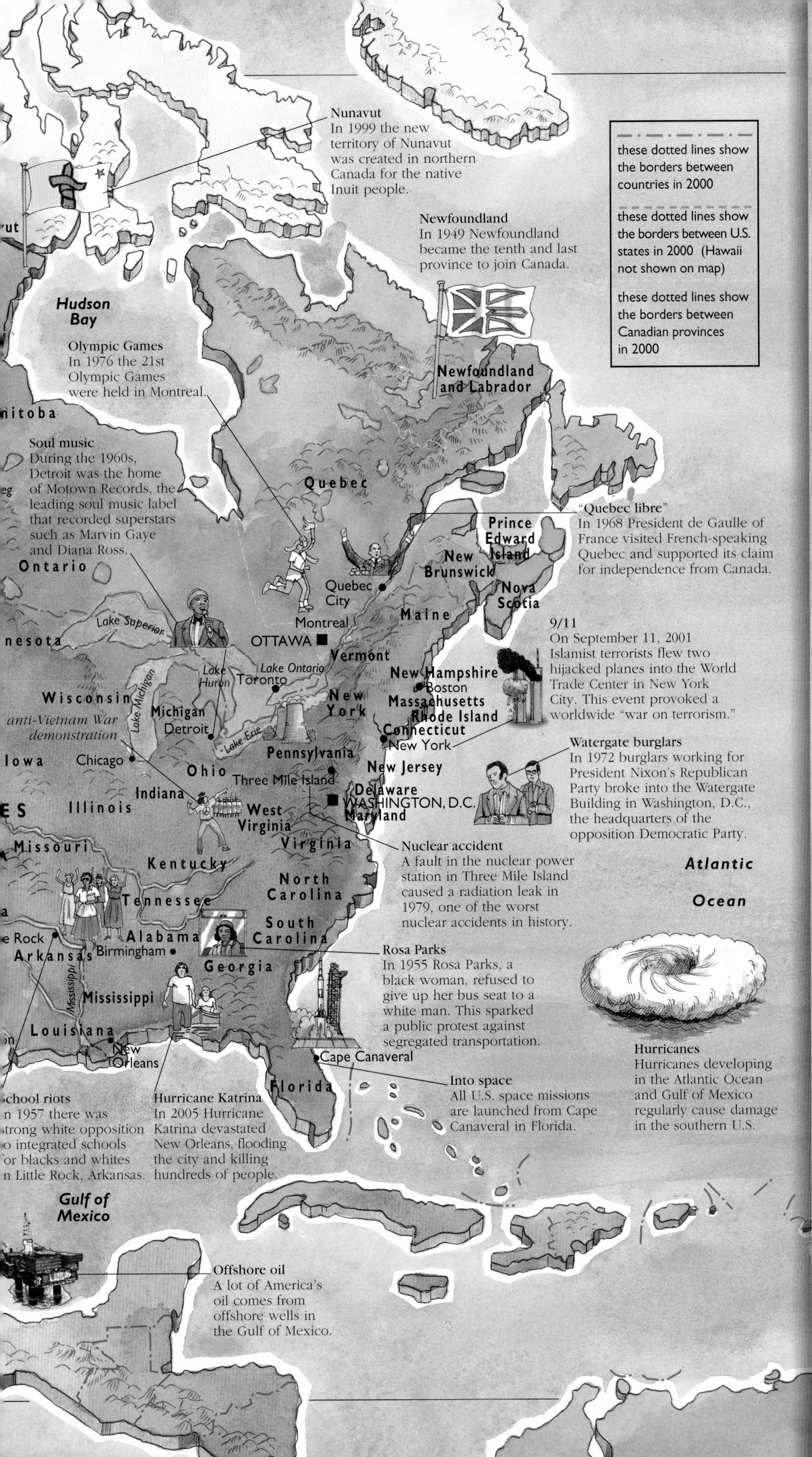
Nunavut
In 1999 the new territory of Nunavut was created in northern Canada for the native Inuit people.
vut
Newfoundland
In 1949 Newfoundland became the tenth and last province to join Canada.
these dotted lines show the borders between countries in 2000
these dotted lines show the borders between U.S. states in 2000 (Hawaii not shown on map)
these dotted lines show the borders between Canadian provinces in 2000
Hudson Bay
Olympic Games
In 1976 the 21st Olympic Games were held in Montreal.
Newfoundland and Labrador
nitoba
Soul music
During the 1960s, Detroit was the home of Motown Records, the leading soul music label that recorded superstars such as Marvin Gaye and Diana Ross.
Quebec
"Quebec libre"
In 1968 President de Gaulle of France visited French-speaking Quebec and supported its claim for independence from Canada.
Prince Edward Island
New Brunswick
Nova Scotia
Ontario
Quebec City
Maine
Montreal
OTTAWA
Lake Superior
nesota
9/11
On September 11, 2001 Islamist terrorists flew two hijacked planes into the World Trade Center in New York City. This event provoked a worldwide "war on terrorism."
Vermont
Lake Ontario
Lake Huron
Toronto
New Hampshire
Boston
Massachusetts
Rhode Island
Connecticut
New York
New York
Wisconsin
Lake Michigan
Michigan
Detroit
anti-Vietnam War demonstration
Lake Erie
Watergate burglars
In 1972 burglars working for President Nixon's Republican Party broke into the Watergate Building in Washington, D.C., the headquarters of the opposition Democratic Party.
Iowa
Chicago
Pennsylvania
Ohio
New Jersey
Three Mile Island
Delaware
WASHINGTON, D.C.
Maryland
Indiana
Illinois
ES
West Virginia
Missouri
Virginia
Nuclear accident
A fault in the nuclear power station in Three Mile Island caused a radiation leak in 1979, one of the worst nuclear accidents in history.
Atlantic Ocean
Kentucky
North Carolina
Tennessee
South Carolina
Alabama
e Rock
Arkansas
Birmingham
Rosa Parks
In 1955 Rosa Parks, a black woman, refused to give up her bus seat to a white man. This sparked a public protest against segregated transportation.
Georgia
Mississippi
Mississippi
Louisiana
New Orleans
Cape Canaveral
Hurricanes
Hurricanes developing in the Atlantic Ocean and Gulf of Mexico regularly cause damage in the southern U.S.
Florida
Into space
All U.S. space missions are launched from Cape Canaveral in Florida.
chool riots
n 1957 there was strong white opposition o integrated schools or blacks and whites n Little Rock, Arkansas.
Hurricane Katrina
In 2005 Hurricane Katrina devastated New Orleans, flooding the city and killing hundreds of people.
Gulf of Mexico
Offshore oil
A lot of America's oil comes from offshore wells in the Gulf of Mexico.

1940–*today*

1940

1945 President Franklin Roosevelt dies in office; Harry Truman takes over the presidency

1945 U.S. and its allies defeat Japan and Germany in World War II

1946 United Nations (UN) organization meets for the first time in New York City

1948 U.S. armed services end racial segregation

1949 U.S. sets up the North Atlantic Treaty Organization (NATO) to defend western Europe against communist aggression

1949 Newfoundland joins Canada

1950

1950 Senator Joe McCarthy starts an anti-communist witchhunt

1950–1953 U.S. troops fight in Korea

1952 Wartime general Dwight D. Eisenhower becomes the president of the U.S.

1954 Supreme Court bans segregated education

1955 Montgomery bus boycott (protest) eventually ends segregated transportation

1957 Federal troops help integrate schools in Arkansas so that black and white students can be educated together

1960

1960 John F. Kennedy is elected as U.S. president

1963 Martin Luther King, Jr. leads a massive civil rights march on Washington, D.C.

1963 President Kennedy is assassinated

1964 Civil Rights Act bans racial discrimination

1965 U.S. sends many troops to Vietnam

1965 Race riots break out in U.S. cities

1968 Martin Luther King, Jr. is assassinated in Memphis, Tennessee

1968 Richard Nixon is elected as U.S. president

1969 U.S. lands first astronauts on the Moon

1970

1972 Watergate break-in

1973 U.S. signs a ceasefire agreement with the North Vietnamese

1974 President Nixon is forced to resign over the Watergate affair

1976 Montreal hosts the Olympic Games

1976 Jimmy Carter is elected as U.S. president

1979 Serious nuclear accident in Three Mile Island

1980

1980 Ronald Reagan is elected as U.S. president

1980 In a referendum (public vote) Quebec narrowly rejects independence from Canada

1981 Reagan survives an assassination attempt

1985 U.S. and U.S.S.R. begin talks to end the Cold War

1987 First limits on nuclear weapons agreed between the U.S. and the U.S.S.R.

1988 George Bush is elected as U.S. president

1990

1991 U.S. troops lead a campaign to end the Iraqi occupation of Kuwait in the Middle East

1992 Bill Clinton is elected as U.S. president

1994 North American Free Trade Agreement between Canada, the U.S., and Mexico

1995 Quebec again rejects independence from Canada in a second referendum

1998 Opponents try but fail to remove President Clinton from office

1999 Nunavut territory is created in northern Canada

2000

2000 George W. Bush is elected as U.S. president

2001 9/11 (September 11) terrorist attacks in New York and Washington, D.C.

2001 U.S.-led invasion of Afghanistan, in response to 9/11, marks the start of the U.S.'s "war on terror"

2003 U.S. and its allies invade Iraq

2005 Hurricane Katrina devastates New Orleans

2010

China in the 1900s

In 1911 the Qing (Manchu) dynasty was overthrown and a republic was established. This led to a long period of civil war and weak government in China. Nationalists, communists, and, after 1937, invading Japanese forces all fought for control of the country. Order was restored when the communists, under Mao Zedong, took power in 1949. They managed to unite the country, although their dictatorial policies caused huge social and economic upheaval. After the death of Mao in 1976, China began to adopt Western economic policies, leading to an economic boom that has made the country one of the richest and most powerful countries in the world today.

RUSSIAN FEDERATION
MONGOLIA
CHINA

The main food
Rice remains the staple diet for most Chinese people. Here, a rice paddy (field) is being prepared for planting.

Population control
To restrict rapid population growth, a limit of "one child per family" was set in 1979. Despite this, the Chinese population today totals 1.32 billion.

Muslim China
The Uygurs of the Xinjiang-Uygur province are Turkic-speaking Muslims. They have more in common with their neighbors in central Asia than they do with the rest of China.

Xinjiang

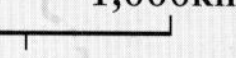
0
1,000km
0
500 miles

The "Great Leap Forward"
In 1958 Mao tried to create a true communist society by setting up huge agricultural communes in which hundreds of peasant farmers would work. The project was a massive failure.

Traditional sports
Despite the rapid modernization and industrialization of China, traditional activities such as flying kites are still very popular.

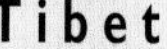
Tibet

Lhasa
NEPAL
INDIA
INDIA
BANGLADESH
MYANMAR (BURMA)

Tibet
Governed by the Dalai Lama from the Potala Palace in Lhasa, Tibet was independent from 1913 until 1950, when Chinese communists occupied the country. A revolt in 1959 failed to regain independence.

Communist China
After they took power in 1949, the Communists used posters, leaflets, banners, and murals to inspire the people to work harder toward achieving a Communist society. This poster from 1965 bore the slogan "Socialism advances in victory everywhere." However, their methods were brutal and not always successful. The Great Leap Forward of 1958–1961 aimed to set up massive farming communes, but it failed and millions of people died of hunger. The Cultural Revolution of 1966–1976 aimed to stamp out old, traditional values so that people could concentrate on revolution. It caused massive social and political disruption.

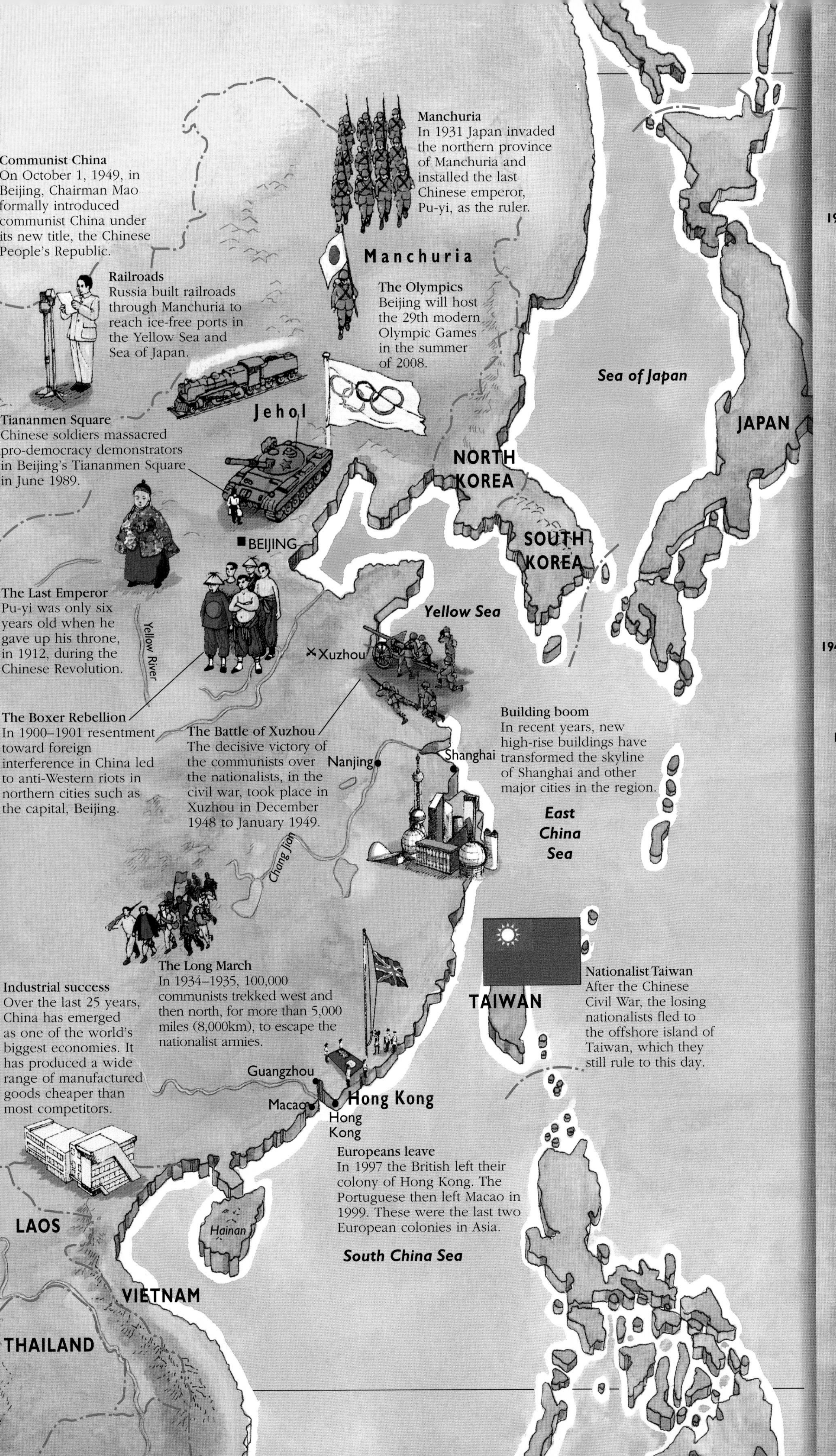
Manchuria
In 1931 Japan invaded the northern province of Manchuria and installed the last Chinese emperor, Pu-yi, as the ruler.
Communist China
On October 1, 1949, in Beijing, Chairman Mao formally introduced communist China under its new title, the Chinese People's Republic.
Manchuria
Railroads
Russia built railroads through Manchuria to reach ice-free ports in the Yellow Sea and Sea of Japan.
The Olympics
Beijing will host the 29th modern Olympic Games in the summer of 2008.
Sea of Japan
Tiananmen Square
Chinese soldiers massacred pro-democracy demonstrators in Beijing's Tiananmen Square in June 1989.
Jehol
JAPAN
NORTH KOREA
SOUTH KOREA
BEIJING
The Last Emperor
Pu-yi was only six years old when he gave up his throne, in 1912, during the Chinese Revolution.
Yellow River
Yellow Sea
Xuzhou
The Boxer Rebellion
In 1900–1901 resentment toward foreign interference in China led to anti-Western riots in northern cities such as the capital, Beijing.
The Battle of Xuzhou
The decisive victory of the communists over the nationalists, in the civil war, took place in Xuzhou in December 1948 to January 1949.
Building boom
In recent years, new high-rise buildings have transformed the skyline of Shanghai and other major cities in the region.
Nanjing
Shanghai
East China Sea
Chang Jian
The Long March
In 1934–1935, 100,000 communists trekked west and then north, for more than 5,000 miles (8,000km), to escape the nationalist armies.
Industrial success
Over the last 25 years, China has emerged as one of the world's biggest economies. It has produced a wide range of manufactured goods cheaper than most competitors.
TAIWAN
Nationalist Taiwan
After the Chinese Civil War, the losing nationalists fled to the offshore island of Taiwan, which they still rule to this day.
Guangzhou
Macao
Hong Kong
Hong Kong
Europeans leave
In 1997 the British left their colony of Hong Kong. The Portuguese then left Macao in 1999. These were the last two European colonies in Asia.
LAOS
Hainan
South China Sea
VIETNAM
THAILAND

1900–*today*

1900

- **1900–1901** Anti-Western riots across northern China
- **1908** Pu-yi becomes the last Qing (Manchu) emperor of China, aged two

1910

- **1911** Nationalists led by Sun Yat-sen overthrow the Qing dynasty and establish a republic
- **1912** Emperor Pu-yi abdicates
- **1913** Tibet becomes independent
- **1917** China falls under the power of local warlords

1920

- **1921** Chinese Communist Party is founded
- **1926** Chiang Kai-shek becomes the Nationalist leader

1930

- **1931** Japanese invade Manchuria
- **1933** Japanese take province of Jehol
- **1934–1935** The Long March
- **1937** Japanese launch full-scale invasion of China; more than 250,000 Chinese civilians are killed as Japanese overrun the Nationalist capital, Nanjing

1940

- **1945** After victory over the Japanese, civil war begins in China between the Nationalists and the Communists
- **1949** Mao Zedong proclaims the Chinese People's Republic in Beijing; Nationalists flee to Taiwan

1950

- **1950** Chinese occupy Tibet
- **1958–1961** The "Great Leap Forward" fails to achieve a true Communist society
- **1959** Tibetan rebellions fail to remove the Chinese

1960

- **1960** China breaks links with the U.S.S.R.
- **1964** China explodes its first atomic weapon
- **1965–1968** Cultural Revolution: Mao urges the Chinese youth to reject the Soviet style of communism; schools are closed, and the movement turns violent as teachers, intellectuals, and others are persecuted

1970

- **1972** U.S. president Nixon visits China
- **1976** Chairman Mao (Mao Zedong) dies
- **1979** "One child per family" policy introduced in China

1980

- **1980** Deng Xiaoping becomes the leader and begins economic reforms
- **1984** Major reforms are introduced to modernize Chinese industry
- **1989** Pro-democracy movement is crushed in Beijing

1990

- **1992** China begins to introduce a "socialist market economy"
- **1997** British return Hong Kong to China
- **1999** Portuguese return Macao to China

2000

- **2007** China becomes the world's third-richest nation, after the U.S. and Japan
- **2008** Beijing hosts the summer Olympic Games

2010

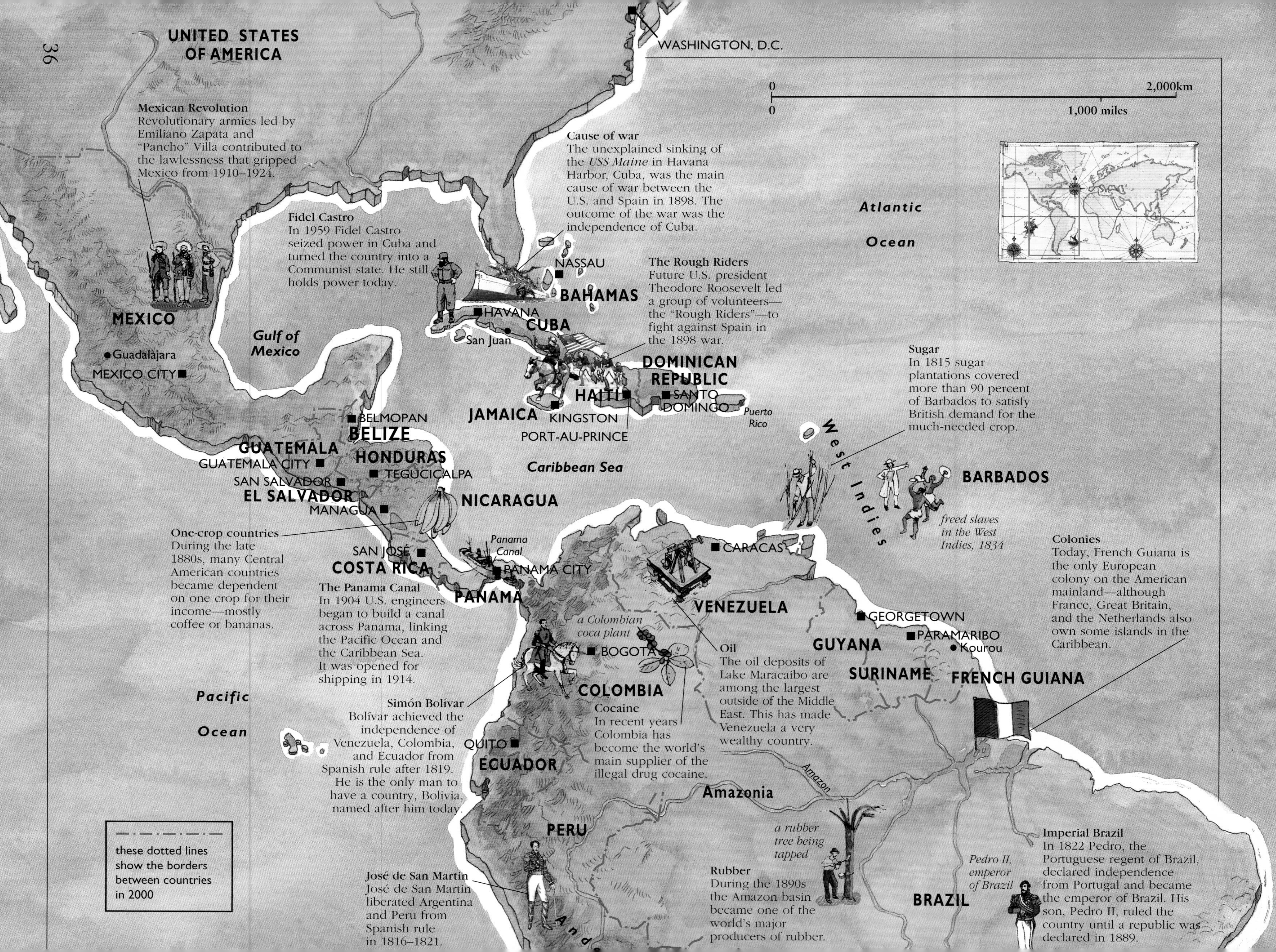
UNITED STATES OF AMERICA
WASHINGTON, D.C.
0 2,000km
0 1,000 miles
Mexican Revolution
Revolutionary armies led by Emiliano Zapata and "Pancho" Villa contributed to the lawlessness that gripped Mexico from 1910–1924.
Cause of war
The unexplained sinking of the *USS Maine* in Havana Harbor, Cuba, was the main cause of war between the U.S. and Spain in 1898. The outcome of the war was the independence of Cuba.
Atlantic Ocean
Fidel Castro
In 1959 Fidel Castro seized power in Cuba and turned the country into a Communist state. He still holds power today.
NASSAU
BAHAMAS
The Rough Riders
Future U.S. president Theodore Roosevelt led a group of volunteers—the "Rough Riders"—to fight against Spain in the 1898 war.
MEXICO
Gulf of Mexico
HAVANA
CUBA
San Juan
Guadalajara
MEXICO CITY
Sugar
In 1815 sugar plantations covered more than 90 percent of Barbados to satisfy British demand for the much-needed crop.
DOMINICAN REPUBLIC
HAITI
SANTO DOMINGO
Puerto Rico
BELMOPAN
BELIZE
JAMAICA
KINGSTON
PORT-AU-PRINCE
West Indies
GUATEMALA
GUATEMALA CITY
HONDURAS
TEGUCICALPA
Caribbean Sea
BARBADOS
SAN SALVADOR
EL SALVADOR
NICARAGUA
MANAGUA
freed slaves in the West Indies, 1834
One-crop countries
During the late 1880s, many Central American countries became dependent on one crop for their income—mostly coffee or bananas.
SAN JOSÉ
COSTA RICA
Panama Canal
PANAMA CITY
CARACAS
Colonies
Today, French Guiana is the only European colony on the American mainland—although France, Great Britain, and the Netherlands also own some islands in the Caribbean.
The Panama Canal
In 1904 U.S. engineers began to build a canal across Panama, linking the Pacific Ocean and the Caribbean Sea. It was opened for shipping in 1914.
PANAMA
VENEZUELA
GEORGETOWN
a Colombian coca plant
BOGOTA
Oil
The oil deposits of Lake Maracaibo are among the largest outside of the Middle East. This has made Venezuela a very wealthy country.
GUYANA
PARAMARIBO
Kourou
SURINAME
FRENCH GUIANA
Pacific Ocean
Simón Bolívar
Bolívar achieved the independence of Venezuela, Colombia, and Ecuador from Spanish rule after 1819. He is the only man to have a country, Bolivia, named after him today.
COLOMBIA
Cocaine
In recent years Colombia has become the world's main supplier of the illegal drug cocaine.
QUITO
ECUADOR
Amazon
Amazonia
these dotted lines show the borders between countries in 2000
PERU
a rubber tree being tapped
Imperial Brazil
In 1822 Pedro, the Portuguese regent of Brazil, declared independence from Portugal and became the emperor of Brazil. His son, Pedro II, ruled the country until a republic was declared in 1889.
Pedro II, emperor of Brazil
José de San Martin
José de San Martin liberated Argentina and Peru from Spanish rule in 1816–1821.
Rubber
During the 1890s the Amazon basin became one of the world's major producers of rubber.
BRAZIL
And

Latin America

Charismatic liberators such as Simón Bolívar helped Latin America win independence from Spain in the early 1800s. The empire of Brazil also gained its independence from Portugal before becoming a republic. All of these new countries were politically unstable and were often governed by dictators. During the 1900s, social divisions between the rich and the poor led to long periods of military rule and revolutionary upheaval. The U.S. supported the continent's independence from European rule but often treated Central American nations as its backyard, controlling their economies and intervening when their elected governments threatened U.S. interests.

The end of slavery

The trade in African slaves across the Atlantic Ocean, to work on the plantations of Central and South America, was ended by Great Britain in 1807 and France in 1815—but a variety of traders continued to supply slaves to Brazil and Cuba until the 1860s. The institution of slavery itself was abolished in all British colonies in 1834 but survived in Brazil until 1888. A lack of alternative work, however, meant that many former slaves were forced to continue working on the plantations as paid laborers.

Bernardo O'Higgins
The liberator of Chile was the son of an Irishman who spent his childhood in Europe. He returned to Chile to lead the struggle for independence after 1813.

Allende
In 1973 a U.S.-backed military coup overthrew President Salvador Allende of Chile, the world's first democratically elected Marxist head of state.

Che Guevara
The revolutionary leader Ernesto "Che" Guevara was killed in Bolivia in 1967 while trying to encourage the tin miners to revolt.

Evita
Juan Péron and his wife Eva (Evita) became very popular leaders in Argentina after 1946.

Brasília
The capital of Brazil was moved from the overcrowded Rio de Janeiro to the new, inland city of Brasília in 1960.

Oil war
The lure of oil in the Gran Chaco region caused war between Bolivia and Paraguay in 1932–1935, although no oil was ever found there.

Immigration
From the mid 1850s, more than 4.5 million immigrants from southern Europe arrived in Argentina. This was followed by 115,000 Jews fleeing from oppression in Russia after 1881.

Gauchos
Cowboys known as gauchos tended the huge cattle ranches in the pampas regions of northern Argentina and Uruguay.

The Falklands
In March 1982 Argentine forces invaded the British-owned Falkland Islands. Three months later they were defeated by British forces.

LA PAZ
BOLIVIA
BRASILIA
PARAGUAY
Gran Chaco
ASUNCIÓN
São Paulo
Rio de Janeiro
CHILE
Andes
SANTIAGO
BUENOS AIRES
URUGUAY
MONTEVIDEO
Pacific Ocean
ARGENTINA
Falkland Islands

1800–2000

1800

1804 Haiti becomes independent from France
1807 Great Britain ends dealings in slave trade
1811 Paraguay is independent from Spain
1819–1922 Simón Bolívar wins independence for Greater Colombia
1821 Mexico and Central America win independence from Spain
1823 U.S. proclaims the Monroe Doctrine, warning European powers not to intervene again in Latin America

1825

1825 Bolivia is independent from Spain
1828 Uruguay is independent from Brazil
1830 Venezuela and Ecuador gain independence from Colombia
1830s Mass immigration from southern Europe to Brazil
1831 Pedro II becomes the emperor of Brazil
1834 Great Britain frees its West Indian slaves
1846–1848 Mexico loses its northern territories in war with the U.S.

1850

1850s Mass immigration from southern Europe to Argentina
1864–1870 War of the Triple Alliance between Paraguay and its neighbors

1875

1879–1883 War of the Pacific: Chile defeats Peru; Bolivia loses access to the sea
1881 Jews flee from persecution in Russia and settle in Argentina
1888 Pedro II abolishes slavery in Brazil
1889 Pedro II is overthrown; Brazil becomes a republic
1898 Spanish-American War: Cuba gains independence from Spain; U.S. gains Puerto Rico

1900

1903 U.S. helps Panama gain independence from Colombia
1910–1924 Mexican Revolution: U.S. intervenes to restore order
1912–1934 U.S. troops police Nicaragua
1914 Panama Canal opens
1917 U.S. gains the Virgin Islands from Denmark

1925

1932–1935 Gran Chaco War between Bolivia and Paraguay
1937–1945 Fascist dictatorship runs Brazil
1940–1942 Ecuador and Peru fight over territories in Amazonia
1946 Juan Péron becomes the president of Argentina

1950

1959 Fidel Castro seizes power in Cuba
1962 Trinidad and Jamaica win independence from Great Britain
1964–1985 Army governs Brazil
1966–1983 Most British colonies gain independence
1973 President Allende of Chile is toppled by a U.S.-backed military coup

1975

1975 Dutch give independence to Suriname
1976–1982 "Dirty war" between the Argentine military and guerilla forces
1984–1990 U.S. supports the Contras against the Nicaraguan government
1988 Mexico joins Canada and U.S. in the North American Free Trade Agreement
1989 Democracy returns to Chile
1998 Hugo Chávez is elected as president of Venezuela and frequently clashes with U.S.

2000

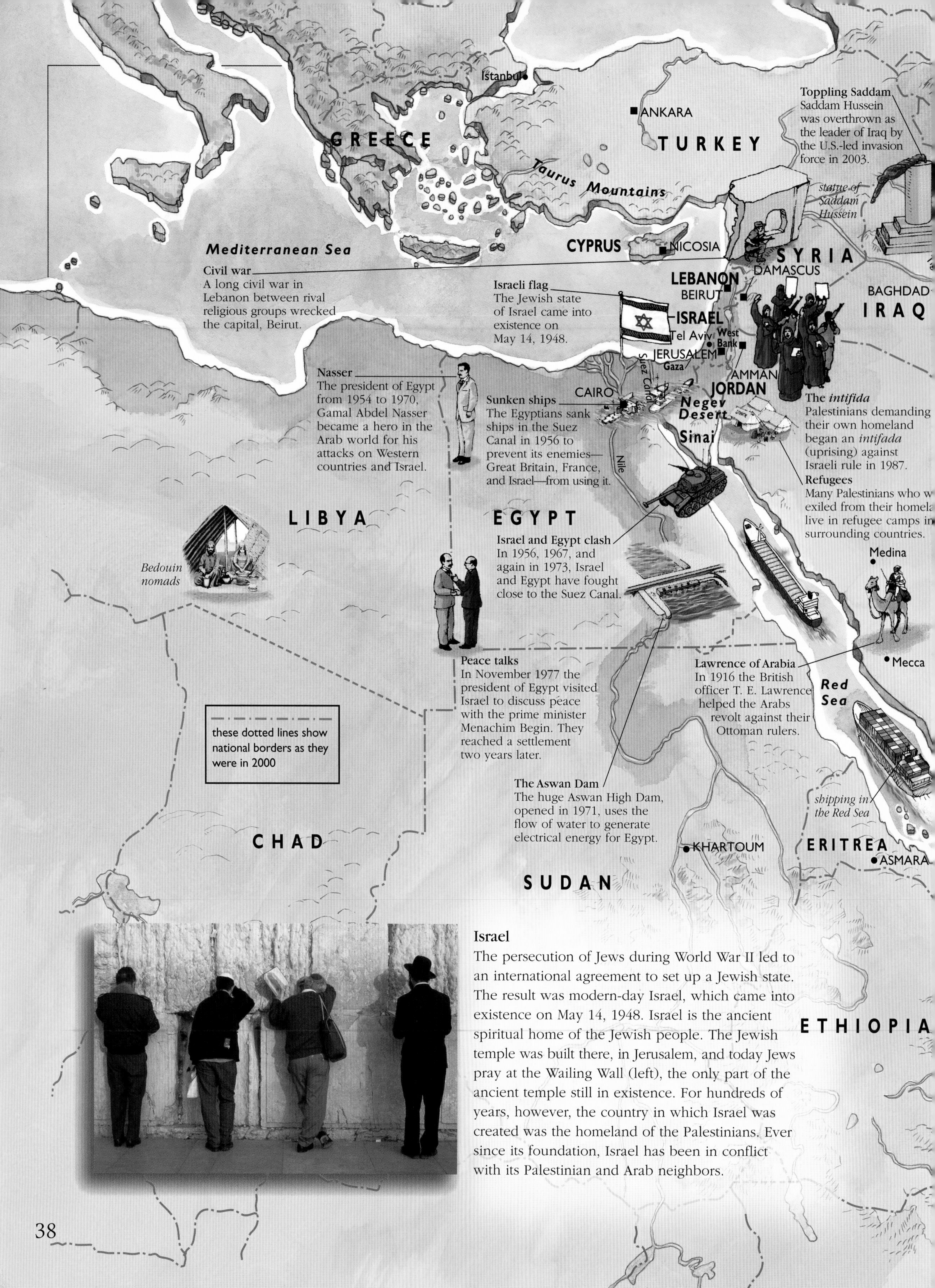
Istanbul
ANKARA
TURKEY
GREECE
Taurus Mountains
Toppling Saddam
Saddam Hussein was overthrown as the leader of Iraq by the U.S.-led invasion force in 2003.
statue of Saddam Hussein
Mediterranean Sea
CYPRUS
NICOSIA
SYRIA
DAMASCUS
Civil war
A long civil war in Lebanon between rival religious groups wrecked the capital, Beirut.
Israeli flag
The Jewish state of Israel came into existence on May 14, 1948.
LEBANON
BEIRUT
ISRAEL
Tel Aviv
West Bank
JERUSALEM
Gaza
AMMAN
JORDAN
BAGHDAD
IRAQ
Nasser
The president of Egypt from 1954 to 1970, Gamal Abdel Nasser became a hero in the Arab world for his attacks on Western countries and Israel.
CAIRO
Suez Canal
Sunken ships
The Egyptians sank ships in the Suez Canal in 1956 to prevent its enemies—Great Britain, France, and Israel—from using it.
Negev Desert
Sinai
Nile
The intifida
Palestinians demanding their own homeland began an intifada (uprising) against Israeli rule in 1987.
Refugees
Many Palestinians who w
exiled from their homel
live in refugee camps in
surrounding countries.
LIBYA
EGYPT
Bedouin nomads
Israel and Egypt clash
In 1956, 1967, and again in 1973, Israel and Egypt have fought close to the Suez Canal.
Medina
Mecca
Peace talks
In November 1977 the president of Egypt visited Israel to discuss peace with the prime minister Menachim Begin. They reached a settlement two years later.
Lawrence of Arabia
In 1916 the British officer T. E. Lawrence helped the Arabs revolt against their Ottoman rulers.
Red Sea
these dotted lines show national borders as they were in 2000
The Aswan Dam
The huge Aswan High Dam, opened in 1971, uses the flow of water to generate electrical energy for Egypt.
shipping in the Red Sea
CHAD
KHARTOUM
ERITREA
ASMARA
SUDAN
ETHIOPIA

Israel

The persecution of Jews during World War II led to an international agreement to set up a Jewish state. The result was modern-day Israel, which came into existence on May 14, 1948. Israel is the ancient spiritual home of the Jewish people. The Jewish temple was built there, in Jerusalem, and today Jews pray at the Wailing Wall (left), the only part of the ancient temple still in existence. For hundreds of years, however, the country in which Israel was created was the homeland of the Palestinians. Ever since its foundation, Israel has been in conflict with its Palestinian and Arab neighbors.

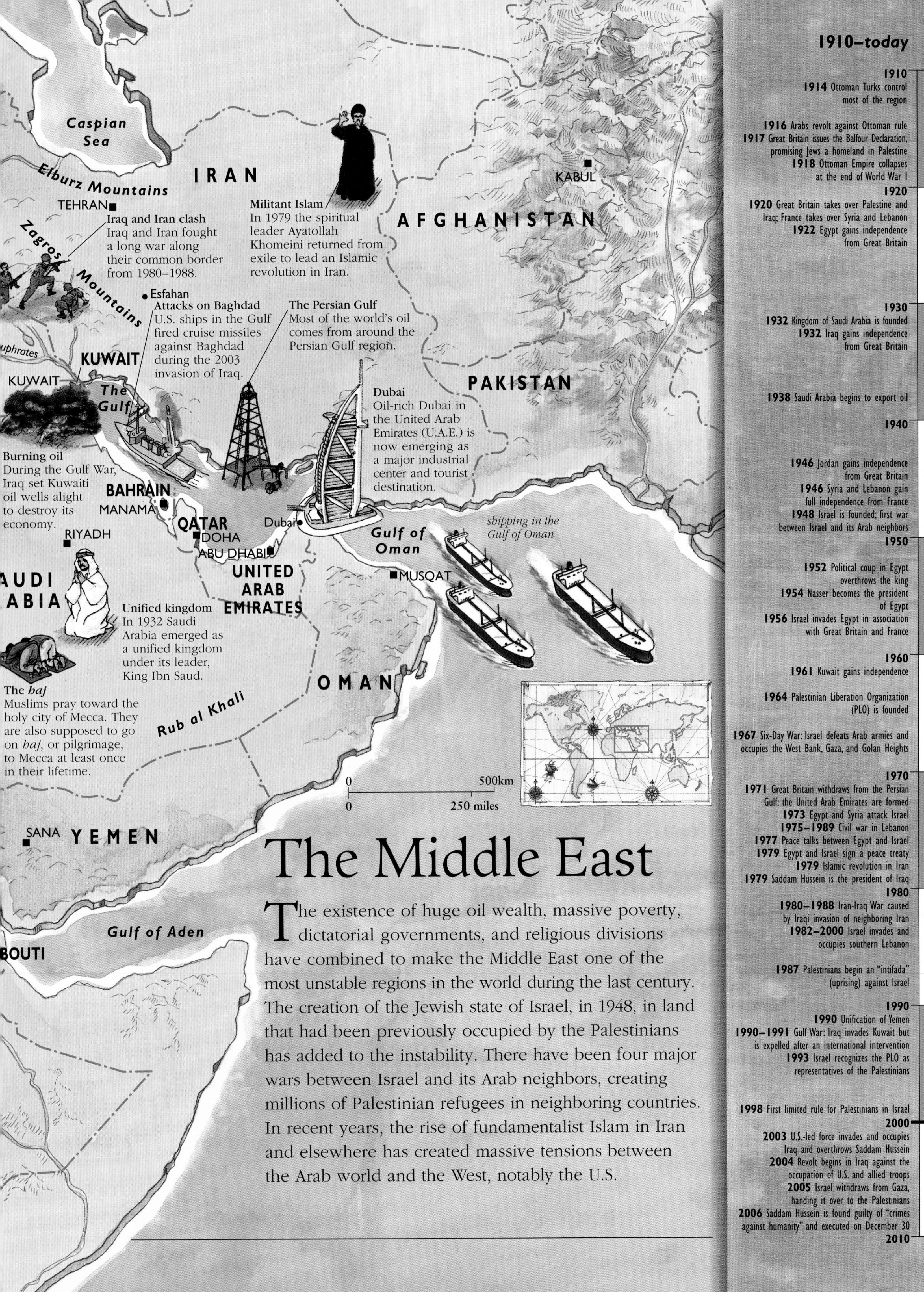
Caspian Sea
Elburz Mountains
IRAN
TEHRAN
Zagros Mountains
Iraq and Iran clash
Iraq and Iran fought a long war along their common border from 1980–1988.
Militant Islam
In 1979 the spiritual leader Ayatollah Khomeini returned from exile to lead an Islamic revolution in Iran.
AFGHANISTAN
KABUL
Esfahan
Attacks on Baghdad
U.S. ships in the Gulf fired cruise missiles against Baghdad during the 2003 invasion of Iraq.
The Persian Gulf
Most of the world's oil comes from around the Persian Gulf region.
uphrates
KUWAIT
KUWAIT
The Gulf
PAKISTAN
Dubai
Oil-rich Dubai in the United Arab Emirates (U.A.E.) is now emerging as a major industrial center and tourist destination.
Burning oil
During the Gulf War, Iraq set Kuwaiti oil wells alight to destroy its economy.
BAHRAIN
MANAMA
QATAR
DOHA
Dubai
ABU DHABI
RIYADH
Gulf of Oman
shipping in the Gulf of Oman
MUSQAT
UNITED ARAB EMIRATES
AUDI ABIA
Unified kingdom
In 1932 Saudi Arabia emerged as a unified kingdom under its leader, King Ibn Saud.
The *haj*
Muslims pray toward the holy city of Mecca. They are also supposed to go on *haj*, or pilgrimage, to Mecca at least once in their lifetime.
OMAN
Rub al Khali
0
500km
0
250 miles
SANA
YEMEN
Gulf of Aden
BOUTI

The Middle East

The existence of huge oil wealth, massive poverty, dictatorial governments, and religious divisions have combined to make the Middle East one of the most unstable regions in the world during the last century. The creation of the Jewish state of Israel, in 1948, in land that had been previously occupied by the Palestinians has added to the instability. There have been four major wars between Israel and its Arab neighbors, creating millions of Palestinian refugees in neighboring countries. In recent years, the rise of fundamentalist Islam in Iran and elsewhere has created massive tensions between the Arab world and the West, notably the U.S.

1910–*today*

1910
1914 Ottoman Turks control most of the region
1916 Arabs revolt against Ottoman rule
1917 Great Britain issues the Balfour Declaration, promising Jews a homeland in Palestine
1918 Ottoman Empire collapses at the end of World War I
1920
1920 Great Britain takes over Palestine and Iraq; France takes over Syria and Lebanon
1922 Egypt gains independence from Great Britain
1930
1932 Kingdom of Saudi Arabia is founded
1932 Iraq gains independence from Great Britain
1938 Saudi Arabia begins to export oil
1940
1946 Jordan gains independence from Great Britain
1946 Syria and Lebanon gain full independence from France
1948 Israel is founded; first war between Israel and its Arab neighbors
1950
1952 Political coup in Egypt overthrows the king
1954 Nasser becomes the president of Egypt
1956 Israel invades Egypt in association with Great Britain and France
1960
1961 Kuwait gains independence
1964 Palestinian Liberation Organization (PLO) is founded
1967 Six-Day War: Israel defeats Arab armies and occupies the West Bank, Gaza, and Golan Heights
1970
1971 Great Britain withdraws from the Persian Gulf: the United Arab Emirates are formed
1973 Egypt and Syria attack Israel
1975–1989 Civil war in Lebanon
1977 Peace talks between Egypt and Israel
1979 Egypt and Israel sign a peace treaty
1979 Islamic revolution in Iran
1979 Saddam Hussein is the president of Iraq
1980
1980–1988 Iran-Iraq War caused by Iraqi invasion of neighboring Iran
1982–2000 Israel invades and occupies southern Lebanon
1987 Palestinians begin an "intifada" (uprising) against Israel
1990
1990 Unification of Yemen
1990–1991 Gulf War: Iraq invades Kuwait but is expelled after an international intervention
1993 Israel recognizes the PLO as representatives of the Palestinians
1998 First limited rule for Palestinians in Israel
2000
2003 U.S.-led force invades and occupies Iraq and overthrows Saddam Hussein
2004 Revolt begins in Iraq against the occupation of U.S. and allied troops
2005 Israel withdraws from Gaza, handing it over to the Palestinians
2006 Saddam Hussein is found guilty of "crimes against humanity" and executed on December 30
2010

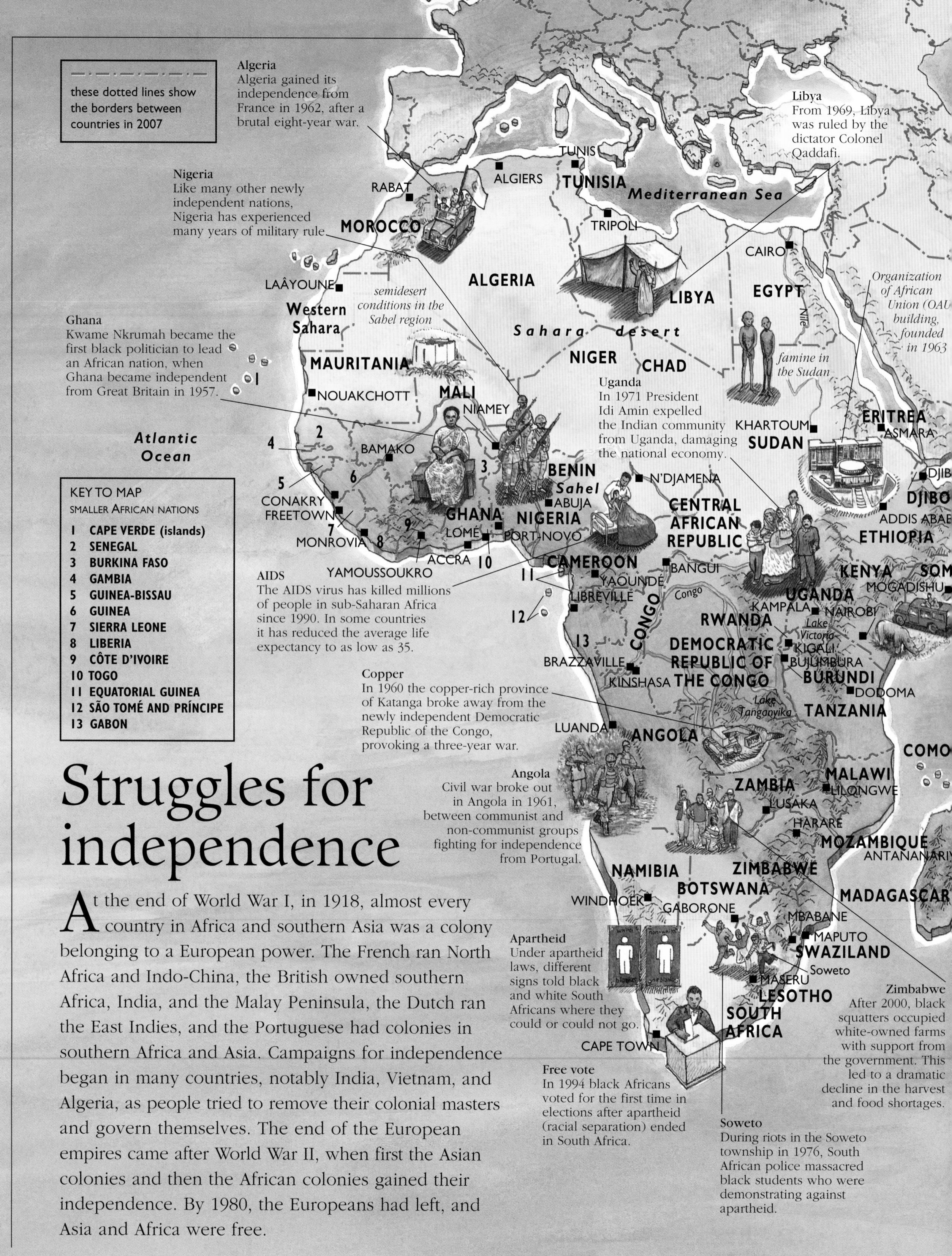

these dotted lines show the borders between countries in 2007
Algeria
Algeria gained its independence from France in 1962, after a brutal eight-year war.
Libya
From 1969, Libya was ruled by the dictator Colonel Qaddafi.
Nigeria
Like many other newly independent nations, Nigeria has experienced many years of military rule.
Ghana
Kwame Nkrumah became the first black politician to lead an African nation, when Ghana became independent from Great Britain in 1957.
Uganda
In 1971 President Idi Amin expelled the Indian community from Uganda, damaging the national economy.
Organization of African Union (OAU) building, founded in 1963
semidesert conditions in the Sahel region
famine in the Sudan
AIDS
The AIDS virus has killed millions of people in sub-Saharan Africa since 1990. In some countries it has reduced the average life expectancy to as low as 35.
Copper
In 1960 the copper-rich province of Katanga broke away from the newly independent Democratic Republic of the Congo, provoking a three-year war.
Angola
Civil war broke out in Angola in 1961, between communist and non-communist groups fighting for independence from Portugal.
Apartheid
Under apartheid laws, different signs told black and white South Africans where they could or could not go.
Free vote
In 1994 black Africans voted for the first time in elections after apartheid (racial separation) ended in South Africa.
Soweto
During riots in the Soweto township in 1976, South African police massacred black students who were demonstrating against apartheid.
Zimbabwe
After 2000, black squatters occupied white-owned farms with support from the government. This led to a dramatic decline in the harvest and food shortages.
KEY TO MAP
SMALLER AFRICAN NATIONS
1 CAPE VERDE (islands)
2 SENEGAL
3 BURKINA FASO
4 GAMBIA
5 GUINEA-BISSAU
6 GUINEA
7 SIERRA LEONE
8 LIBERIA
9 CÔTE D'IVOIRE
10 TOGO
11 EQUATORIAL GUINEA
12 SÃO TOMÉ AND PRÍNCIPE
13 GABON
Atlantic Ocean
Mediterranean Sea
Sahara desert
Sahel
Nile
Congo
Lake Victoria
Lake Tanganyika
RABAT
ALGIERS
TUNIS
TUNISIA
TRIPOLI
CAIRO
MOROCCO
ALGERIA
LIBYA
EGYPT
LAÂYOUNE
Western Sahara
MAURITANIA
NOUAKCHOTT
MALI
NIAMEY
NIGER
CHAD
SUDAN
KHARTOUM
ERITREA
ASMARA
DJIBOUTI
ADDIS ABABA
ETHIOPIA
BAMAKO
BENIN
N'DJAMENA
ABUJA
NIGERIA
GHANA
CONAKRY
FREETOWN
MONROVIA
LOMÉ
PORT-NOVO
ACCRA
YAMOUSSOUKRO
CENTRAL AFRICAN REPUBLIC
CAMEROON
YAOUNDÉ
BANGUI
LIBREVILLE
CONGO
KENYA
MOGADISHU
UGANDA
KAMPALA
NAIROBI
RWANDA
KIGALI
BUJUMBURA
BURUNDI
DEMOCRATIC REPUBLIC OF THE CONGO
BRAZZAVILLE
KINSHASA
DODOMA
TANZANIA
LUANDA
ANGOLA
COMOROS
ZAMBIA
MALAWI
LILONGWE
LUSAKA
HARARE
MOZAMBIQUE
ANTANANARIVO
NAMIBIA
ZIMBABWE
BOTSWANA
MADAGASCAR
WINDHOEK
GABORONE
MBABANE
MAPUTO
SWAZILAND
Soweto
MASERU
LESOTHO
SOUTH AFRICA
CAPE TOWN

Struggles for independence

At the end of World War I, in 1918, almost every country in Africa and southern Asia was a colony belonging to a European power. The French ran North Africa and Indo-China, the British owned southern Africa, India, and the Malay Peninsula, the Dutch ran the East Indies, and the Portuguese had colonies in southern Africa and Asia. Campaigns for independence began in many countries, notably India, Vietnam, and Algeria, as people tried to remove their colonial masters and govern themselves. The end of the European empires came after World War II, when first the Asian colonies and then the African colonies gained their independence. By 1980, the Europeans had left, and Asia and Africa were free.

Kashmir
Ever since their independence in 1947, Pakistan and India have frequently fought over the Kashmir region.

Amritsar
The killing of 379 Indians by British troops in 1919 increased support for Indian independence from Great Britain.

Bangladesh
Bangladesh became independent from the rest of Pakistan in 1971. Its low-lying land is often flooded by the ocean.

Cambodia
After 1975, the Khmer Rouge—a hard-line communist government—murdered more than two million people in Cambodia, before it was expelled in 1979.

Vietnam
Communist soldiers first fought the French and then the Americans before Vietnam was finally united under their rule in 1975.

ISLAMABAD
Kashmir
Himalayas
Quetta
Delhi
NEPAL
THIMPHU
PAKISTAN
KATHMANDU
BHUTAN
Indus
Ganges
NEW DELHI
DHAKA
Karachi
INDIA
Calcutta
MYANMAR (BURMA)
HANOI
East China Sea
Mumbai (Bombay)
BANGLADESH
LAOS
VIENTIANE
Bay of Bengal
YANGON (RANGOON)
VIETNAM
MANILA
Chennai (Madras)
CAMBODIA
PHILIPPINES
PHNOM PENH
South China Sea
Arabian Sea
SRI LANKA
Kuala Lumpur
MALAYSIA
SINGAPORE
INDONESIA
JAKARTA
SEYCHELLES
Indian Ocean
MAURITIUS
AUSTRALIA

Partition
When India became independent in 1947, millions of Muslims fled for their lives into neighboring Pakistan. The Hindus fled in the opposite direction.

the Asian tsunami of 2004

the Petronas Towers in Kuala Lumpur, Malaysia

logging in Indonesia

Nehru
Pandit Nehru led India to independence and became its first prime minister. He led the country until his death in 1964.

Malaysia
Since its independence in 1957, Malaysia has become one of the richest countries in the world, with many impressive, high-rise buildings.

Tamil Tigers
Since 1983 the minority Tamils have fought a vicious civil war for independence from the majority Sinhalese people of Sri Lanka.

Singapore
The island of Singapore became independent from Malaysia in 1965 and has now developed as a major shipping port for the entire region.

East Timor
In 2002 the former Portuguese colony of East Timor finally gained its independence after Indonesia occupied the country in 1975.

0 — 3,000km
0 — 1,500 miles

Indian independence

The struggle for Indian independence from British rule was led by the Congress Party, among whose leaders was Mahatma Gandhi. In 1930 Gandhi led a symbolic march to the ocean, where he picked up salt. This broke the British government's control over the production of salt and made British rule look stupid in the process. These and other peaceful protests eventually forced the British to leave India, which was partitioned in 1947 between Muslim Pakistan and the mostly Hindu India.

1910–*today*

1910

1918 World War I ends
1918 Most of Africa and southern and southeast Asia are under European colonial rule
1920 Great Britain, France, and South Africa take over former German colonies in Africa
1922 Egypt gains independence from Great Britain
1926 Morocco revolts against French rule

1930

1935 Great Britain grants home rule to Indian provinces
1935–1936 Italy invades Abyssinia (Ethiopia)
1940–1941 Japan occupies French Indo-China
1941 Great Britain occupies Italian east African colonies and frees Abyssinia
1941 Ho Chi Minh forms a nationalist Viet Minh guerilla group in Vietnam
1941–1942 Japan occupies southeast Asia
1946 Philippines is independent of the U.S.
1946–1954 French fight Viet Minh for control of Vietnam
1947 Great Britain grants independence to India and Pakistan
1948 Great Britain grants independence to Burma (Myanmar) and Ceylon (Sri Lanka)
1949 Dutch grant Indonesia independence

1950

1951 Libya becomes independent
1954 France leaves Indo-China; Laos and Cambodia become independent
1955 Sudan gains independence from joint British-Egyptian rule
1956 France grants independence to Morocco and Tunisia
1957 Great Britain grants the Malay Peninsula independence
1957 Ghana becomes the first independent black African nation
1960–1962 Most of sub-Saharan is independent
1962 France grants Algeria independence
1963 Federation of Malaysia is created
1964–1975 U.S. supports South Vietnam against communist North Vietnam
1965 Singapore independent of Malaysia

1970

1971 Bangladesh breaks away from Pakistan
1975 Indonesia occupies the Portuguese colony of East Timor
1975 Vietnam is reunited under communist rule
1975 Portuguese colonies in Africa win independence, but civil war continues in Angola
1975–1979 Khmer Rouge military regime kills millions in Cambodia
1980 Zimbabwe, Great Britain's last remaining colony in Africa, wins independence
1983 Tamil Tiger guerillas begin their fight for independence in Sri Lanka

1990

1990 Namibia gains independence from South Africa
1993 Eritrea gains independence from Ethiopia
1994 Apartheid (racial segregation) comes to an end in South Africa; Nelson Mandela is elected as president of South Africa
1994 Genocide (mass extermination of native people) in Rwanda by extremist militia groups
2002 East Timor gains independence from Indonesia
2002 Civil war ends in Angola after a ceasefire is arranged
2004 Tsunami devastates coastal regions around the Indian Ocean

2010

Modern Europe

In 1945, after the defeat of Germany at the end of World War II, Europe became divided into two parts. The communist east contained countries that were occupied by Soviet troops, while the capitalist west was home to democratic countries. This division of Europe—known as the Iron Curtain—lasted until 1990, when communism collapsed in the east and democratic governments took over. The U.S.S.R. itself collapsed the following year and divided into 15 separate countries. Since then, most of Europe has become more united within the European Union, although huge economic differences still exist between the poorer east and the wealthier west.

The Berlin Wall
In 1989 the wall that divided communist East Berlin from capitalist West Berlin was pulled down. The city was reunited.
Female prime minister
In 1979 Margaret Thatcher became the first female prime minister of Great Britain (also, officially, known as the United Kingdom).
North Sea
NORWAY
SWEDE
OSLO
STOCKH
The Nuremburg trials
Twenty-one leading Nazis were put on trial in 1946 for war crimes. Eleven of them were sentenced to death.
DENMARK
COPENHAGEN
Shipping
Rotterdam is Europe's busiest port.
"The Troubles"
Irish republican opposition to British rule in Northern Ireland erupted into violence in 1969.
Northern Ireland
DUBLIN
IRELAND
UNITED KINGDOM
these dotted lines show the borders in Europe in 2007
AMSTERDAM
NETHERLANDS
Rotterdam
BERLIN
LONDON
BELGIUM
GERMANY
BRUSSELS
The Channel Tunnel
A rail tunnel link under the English Channel, between England and France, opened in 1994.
PRAGU
CZECH
English Channel
LUXEMBOURG
0
500km
0
250 miles
Fishing
Industrial fishing by European trawler fleets has seriously depleted fish stocks in recent years.
PARIS
FRANCE
VIE
KEY TO MAP
SMALLER EUROPEAN NATIONS
1 SLOVENIA
2 CROATIA
3 BOSNIA AND HERZEGOVINA
4 SERBIA
5 MONTENEGRO
6 MACEDONIA
The May Uprising
In 1968 riots erupted between students and police in France.
Farm power
Farmers have huge political and economic influence in modern-day France.
BERN
Alps
AUSTRI
SWITZERLAND
LJUBLJANA
ZAG
Democracy triumphs
In 1981 Colonel Molina tried to end democracy in Spain by storming the parliament. He failed.
Pyrenees
Corsica
ITALY
European Union
In 1957 six countries signed the Treaty of Rome, setting up the European Economic Community (EEC).
ROME
SPAIN
Atlantic Ocean
PORTUGAL
MADRID
LISBON
Vacation destination
Since the 1950s, mass tourism has brought great wealth to large parts of Spain.
Balearic Islands
Sardinia
Revolution of the Flowers
A military coup in Portugal in 1974 overthrew almost 50 years of dictatorship and brought democracy back to the country.
Mediterranean Sea
Sicily
Ma

The European Union

France and Germany had gone to war with each other in 1870, 1914, and 1939. After 1945, they decided to live together in peace. In 1952 the two countries, along with Italy and the "Benelux" nations (Belgium, Luxembourg, and the Netherlands), merged their coal and steel industries. The six then set up the European Economic Community (EEC) in 1957. Great Britain joined in 1973, and eight more countries by 1995. Today, the European Union, as it is now called, has 27 members, a single currency (for almost all members), and its own parliament and laws.

Solidarity
The independent "Solidarity" trade union took on and defeated the communists in Poland in the 1980s.

Seeking peace
In 1970 the West German chancellor Willy Brandt went to Warsaw, in Poland, to seek peace between eastern and western Europe.

Reforming communism
Mikhail Gorbachev tried to reform the communist U.S.S.R. after 1985, but he could not prevent its collapse in 1991.

Nuclear catastrophe
In 1986 a reactor exploded at the Chernobyl nuclear power station, close to Kiev. It remains the worst nuclear accident in history.

Chechnya
Russia invaded the breakaway republic of Chechnya in 1994–1996. The war has wrecked the Chechen capital, Grozny.

Ukraine
The Orange Revolution in the Ukraine in 2004 overturned the results of a rigged presidential election and handed power to the democratic opposition.

Democracy
After the collapse of communism in 1989, voters across eastern Europe elected democratic governments.

Romania
One of the worst communist dictators was Nicolae Ceausescu of Romania, who erected massive public buildings throughout the country.

Georgia
The Rose Revolution of 2004 introduced democracy to Georgia for the first time since its independence from the U.S.S.R. in 1991.

Oil supplies
In 2005 an oil pipeline was opened, taking oil from Baku on the Caspian Sea, through Georgia and Turkey, to Ceyhan on the Mediterranean coast.

The Olympics
The Olympic Games returned to their spiritual home in Greece when Athens hosted the games in 2004.

Cyprus
UN (United Nations) troops keep Greeks and Turks apart on the divided island of Cyprus.

War in Bosnia
A vicious civil war from 1992–1995 led to atrocities against ethnic minorities in Bosnia.

FINLAND HELSINKI TALLINN ESTONIA LATVIA RIGA LITHUANIA VILNIUS MINSK BELARUS MOSCOW RUSSIAN FEDERATION WARSAW KIEV UKRAINE SLOVAKIA MOLDOVA CHIŞINĂU BUDAPEST HUNGARY ROMANIA BUCHAREST BELGRADE BULGARIA SOFIA Black Sea Chechnya Caucasus GEORGIA PODGORICA SKOPJE TIRANË ALBANIA Istanbul TURKEY ANKARA Ceyhan GREECE ATHENS NICOSIA CYPRUS Crete Mediterranean Sea

1945–*today*

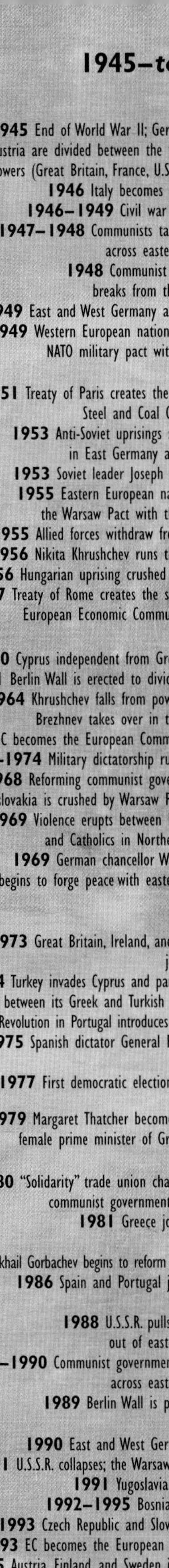

1940

1945 End of World War II; Germany and Austria are divided between the four Allied powers (Great Britain, France, U.S., U.S.S.R.)
1946 Italy becomes a republic
1946–1949 Civil war in Greece
1947–1948 Communists take control across eastern Europe
1948 Communist Yugoslavia breaks from the U.S.S.R.
1949 East and West Germany are created
1949 Western European nations sign the NATO military pact with the U.S.

1950

1951 Treaty of Paris creates the European Steel and Coal Community
1953 Anti-Soviet uprisings suppressed in East Germany and Poland
1953 Soviet leader Joseph Stalin dies
1955 Eastern European nations sign the Warsaw Pact with the U.S.S.R.
1955 Allied forces withdraw from Austria
1956 Nikita Khrushchev runs the U.S.S.R.
1956 Hungarian uprising crushed by Soviets
1957 Treaty of Rome creates the six-member European Economic Community (EEC)

1960

1960 Cyprus independent from Great Britain
1961 Berlin Wall is erected to divide the city
1964 Khrushchev falls from power; Leonid Brezhnev takes over in the U.S.S.R.
1967 EEC becomes the European Community (EC)
1967–1974 Military dictatorship rules Greece
1968 Reforming communist government in Czechoslovakia is crushed by Warsaw Pact troops
1969 Violence erupts between Protestants and Catholics in Northern Ireland
1969 German chancellor Willy Brandt begins to forge peace with eastern Europe

1970

1973 Great Britain, Ireland, and Denmark join the EC
1974 Turkey invades Cyprus and partitions the island between its Greek and Turkish inhabitants
1974 Revolution in Portugal introduces democracy
1975 Spanish dictator General Franco dies
1977 First democratic elections in Spain
1979 Margaret Thatcher becomes the first female prime minister of Great Britain

1980

1980 "Solidarity" trade union challenges the communist government in Poland
1981 Greece joins the EC
1985 Mikhail Gorbachev begins to reform the U.S.S.R.
1986 Spain and Portugal join the EC
1988 U.S.S.R. pulls its troops out of eastern Europe
1989–1990 Communist governments collapse across eastern Europe
1989 Berlin Wall is pulled down

1990

1990 East and West Germany unite
1991 U.S.S.R. collapses; the Warsaw Pact ends
1991 Yugoslavia falls apart
1992–1995 Bosnian civil war
1993 Czech Republic and Slovakia divide
1993 EC becomes the European Union (EU)
1995 Austria, Finland, and Sweden join the EU
1998 Good Friday Agreement brings peace to Northern Ireland
1999 Former communist nations in eastern Europe join NATO

2000

2002 A single European currency, the "euro," is introduced in 12 EU states
2004 Athens hosts the Olympic Games
2004 EU enlarges to 25 member states
2005 Irish Republican Army (IRA) ends the armed struggle in Northern Ireland
2006 Montenegro votes for independence from Serbia
2007 Romania and Bulgaria join the EU, bringing the total number of democratic member states to 27

2010

The world today:
Looking toward the future

The world at the beginning of the new millennium is an incredibly challenging place. Rapid population growth—there are at least 6.4 billion people squashed onto the planet today—and industrial development are straining the world's resources and leading to environmental disasters. Millions of people have left their homes in search of wealth and happiness, creating social and economic problems in both the countries that they have left and those where they have settled. Tensions exist between the rich and the poor and between people of different religious faiths. But there are also many ways in which human beings are dealing with these challenges and trying to solve the problems of the modern world.

Multiculturalism
In the last 50 years large numbers of people left poverty and often oppression in poorer parts of the world and moved to the rich nations of Europe, North America, and Australia in search of work and a better life. These migrants took their own religions and cultures with them, turning their host cities into vibrant multicultural, multiethnic places. While they have benefited economically, many migrants have faced racial hatred and social isolation in their new countries. This picture (above) shows children participating in the Free Time arts festival, held every summer in London, England. The festival is organized by artists from a wide variety of cultures.

A large percentage of the world's population now lives in heavily built-up urban environments. This is the sprawling city of Los Angeles in California.

AIDS awareness

During the 1980s a new disease—AIDS, or Acquired Immune Deficiency Syndrome—spread around the world. There is no known cure for the disease, although an expensive combination of drugs can slow down its progress. More than 40 million people now have AIDS, the vast majority of them living in Africa and Asia. Its effect on poorer countries is immense, reducing the overall life expectancy of the population and creating many thousands of orphaned or sick children such as this baby in Soweto, South Africa (left).

Charity groups working in Africa and Asia have set up projects to help children whose parents have died from AIDS.

Every year, World AIDS Day aims to raise awareness about the disease and raise money for sufferers. Here, Chinese students are participating in fundraising activities.

Sustainable development

The huge increase in the world's population over the last 50 years, and the rapid economic growth of previously poor countries such as India and China (above), have together put a strain on the world's natural resources such as oil, gas, and water. Environmentalists, aid workers, and economists are now looking at ways in which economic development can sustain rather than exploit these resources for the benefit of future generations.

Alternative energy sources

It has become obvious that humans are having a harmful impact on the world's climate. Pollution from cars, airplanes, and industry have contributed to a steady rise in temperatures. This may result in the melting of icecaps and glaciers, causing sea levels to rise and flood many low-lying parts of the world. "Renewable" forms of energy, such as wind power (below), are being used more, because they do not produce any of the "greenhouse gases" that contribute to global warming.

Huge rows of windmills are now a common sight in isolated or mountainous locations such as the Tehachapi Pass in California. Wind farms have been generating electricity in this region since the early 1980s.

Index

This index lists the main peoples, places, and topics that you will find in this book. It is not a full index of all the place names and physical features to be found on the maps.

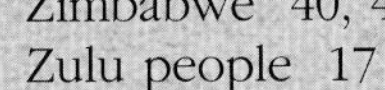

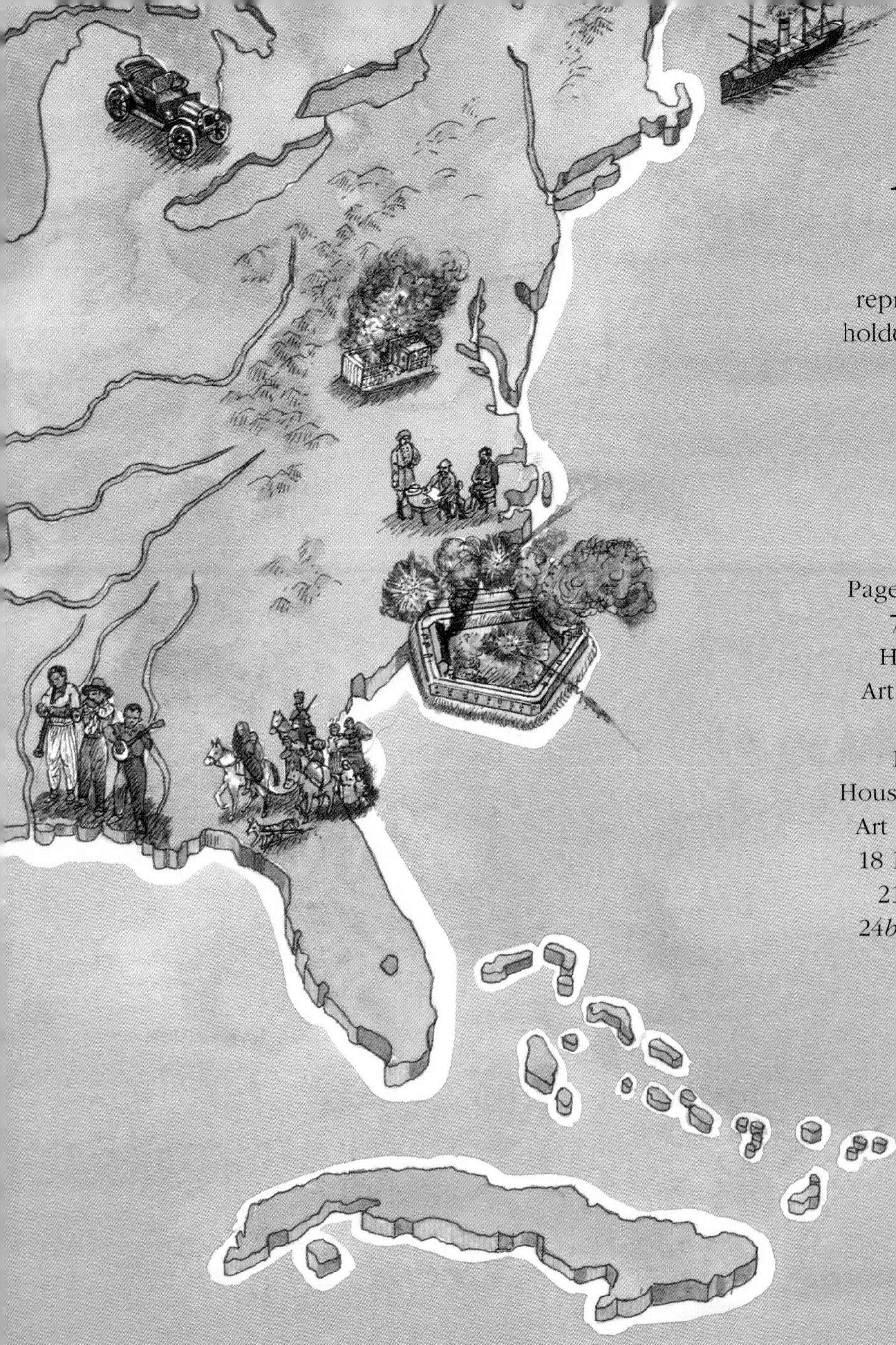

Acknowledgments

The publisher would like to thank the following for permission to reproduce their material. Every care has been taken to trace copyright holders. However, if there have been unintentional omissions or failure to trace copyright holders, we apologize and will, if informed, endeavor to make corrections in any future edition.

Key: *b* = bottom, *c* = center, *l* = left, *r* = right, *t* = top

Pages 6*tl* and 6*c* Corbis/Bettmann; 6*b* Corbis/epa; 7*l* Corbis/Ron Watts; 7*r* Alamy/Jan Tadeusz; 7*ctr* Alamy/Tetra Images; 7*cbr* Alamy/David Hancock; 8 Art Archive/Musée du Louvre/Dagli Orti; 10*t* Bridgeman Art Library/Dallas Historical Society; 10*b* Bridgeman Art Library/Leeds Museums & Art Galleries; 11*tl* Getty/Hulton Archive; 11*c* Heritage Image Partnership/Topfoto/Ann Ronan; 11*b* Getty/George Eastman House; 12 Bridgeman Art Library/V&A Museum, London; 14 Bridgeman Art Library/Medford Historical Society Collection; 17 Corbis/Bettmann; 18 Bridgeman Art Library/Musée de la ville de Paris/Archive Charmet; 21 Corbis; 22 Corbis/Sygma/Thomas Johnson; 24*tl* Corbis/Bettmann; 24*bl* Getty/Savill; 24*br* Corbis/Sunset Boulevard; 25*t* Corbis/Bettmann; 25*b* Corbis/Underwood & Underwood; 26 Corbis/Hulton-Deutsch Collection; 28 Corbis; 31 Getty/Tom Stoddart; 32 Getty/AFP; 34 Corbis/Swim Ink 2; 37 Art Archive/Musée du Chateau de Versailles; 38 Art Archive/The Travel Site; 41 Getty/Keystone; 43 Getty Gerard Cerles; 44*tr* Corbis/Gideon Mendel; 44*b* Getty Toyohiro Yamada; 45*tl* Getty Per-Anders Pettersson; 45*cl* Getty Images; 45*cr* Corbis/Reuters/Nir Elias; 45*b* Getty/National Geographic Society/Marc Moritsch.

The publisher would like to thank the following illustrators: Cover and page 1 Mark Bergin; additional illustrations on pages 16, 17, 18, 19, 32, and 33 also by Mark Bergin. All other illustrations by Kevin Maddison.